A Field Guide to
Nature as Spiritual Practice

A Field Guide to
Nature as Spiritual Practice

Steven Chase

William B. Eerdmans Publishing Company
Grand Rapids, Michigan / Cambridge, U.K.

Published 2011 by
Wm. B. Eerdmans Publishing Co.
2140 Oak Industrial Drive N.E., Grand Rapids, Michigan 49505 /
P.O. Box 163, Cambridge CB3 9PU U.K.

Printed in the United States of America

16 15 14 13 12 11   7 6 5 4 3 2 1

Library of Congress Cataloging-in-Publication Data

Chase, Steven.
    A field guide to nature as spiritual practice / Steven Chase.
        p.   cm.
    ISBN 978-0-8028-6652-3 (pbk.: alk. paper)
    1. Nature — Religious aspects — Christianity. 2. Spiritual life —
Christianity.   I. Title.

    BR115.N3C43   2011
    248 — dc22

                                            2011009862

www.eerdmans.com

Contents

Using the *Field Guide to Nature as Spiritual Practice*

Woven together, Christian practices form a way of life. . . . [Practices are] like a tree whose branches reach out toward the future, even when the earth is shaking, because it is nourished by living water.

Craig Dykstra and Dorothy C. Bass, in *Practicing Our Faith*[1]

Many fine books — both ancient and contemporary — have been written about practice and spiritual formation. Many equally fine books have been written on a wide range of topics having to do with creation, earth, and nature. Together, *Nature as Spiritual Practice* and the *Field Guide to Nature as Spiritual Practice* differ from these in presenting both theological/scriptural/historical/cultural discussions of creation and nature-practice.

In this book I interweave the text (theory) of *Nature as Spiritual Practice* and the practice in both *Nature as Spiritual Practice* and the *Field Guide* to reflect an ancient partnership grounded in Greek philosophy, later assimilated in new ways by early mothers and fathers of the Christian church, and today undergoing a long-neglected retrieval and revival. Practice deepens reflective, critical theory at the same time that theory deepens experiential practice. Together they engage mind, body, and spirit in a holistic way that leaves us open and receptive to the dynamics of change, need, desire, and renewal. This is especially true with regard to the formational quality of the

---

1. Craig Dykstra and Dorothy C. Bass, "A Way of Thinking about a Way of Life," in *Practicing Our Faith: A Way of Life for a Searching People,* ed. Dorothy C. Bass (San Francisco: Jossey-Bass, 1997), 203.

1

natural world, where, as Bass and Dykstra suggest, participative practices are organic ways of thinking about and experiencing creation as what in fact creation is: a way of life.

Field Guides

Traditionally field guides are books designed to help seek out, find, and identify particular aspects of creation. There are, for instance, field guides to help find and identify birds (some by region or song), shells, butterflies, rocks and minerals, animal tracks, trees and shrubs, reptiles and amphibians, wildflowers, stars and planets, insects, edible plants, fishes, weather and clouds, geological forms or structures, mushrooms, and much more. Most are keyed to particular locations and obvious identifying marks, and the details provided, depending on the field guide, may include seasons, habitat, species, identifying shapes, colors, sounds and habits, food sources, means of reproduction, means of identifying similar species, and again, much more. In themselves, field guides are wonderful ways to get out in nature, to begin observing closely, or simply to wander — often noticing characteristics or other aspects of nature within a particular habitat. It is very difficult, for instance, to use a field guide for wildflowers and not notice things like butterflies, insects, seeds, soil composition, birds, and much more.

The Field Guide to Nature as Spiritual Practice functions in a similar way to any field guide. It will get you into nature; it will encourage you to pay attention to details large and small; it will awaken curiosity; it will invite you to reacquaint yourself with wonder and astonishment and beauty in nature; it will lead you into wanderings, serendipitous experiences, surprises, perhaps even into getting lost; and it will inform your decisions about how to live responsibly and with care on the earth on which you walk. (Just don't take a nap in the poison ivy!) The *Field Guide* is designed to be taken with you into the "field."

A Word on the Practices[2]

Whether you or I notice it or not, we are always situated in some place within creation. Though contemporary culture does its best to make cre-

2. See Appendix A in *Nature as Spiritual Practice* on the nature of specifically Christian practice.

ation more predictable, at any moment in any place, creation is still capable of shifting, even shattering, our expectations. This organic patterning and chaotic potential are a part of what makes creation such a good teacher. And it is also the reason why each of the practices in this book begins with an "intention." Beginning with an "intention," the practices never have a goal; the shifts and patterns and potentials of nature also preclude a goal. As a first practice, you might ask yourself, "What is the goal of creation?" The practices are suggestions, experiments in spiritual formation, invitations. After the "intention," nature becomes its own adventure.

Using *Nature as Spiritual Practice* and the *Field Guide* Together

NOTE ON ORGANIZATION: In *Nature as Spiritual Practice,* about one-quarter of the suggested practices are given in full. The "title" of the practice and the "intention" of each practice not given in full is also included in *Nature as Spiritual Practice.* The *Field Guide* contains all of the practices in complete form: those given in full in *Nature as Spiritual Practice* and the complete practice for which only the "title" and "intention" are given in *Nature as Spiritual Practice.* You will find that the full practices in the *Field Guide* are arranged in the order you find them in *Nature as Spiritual Practice,* and they are keyed numerically according to the chapters. The arrangement of text and practices will give you maximum flexibility for reading, practice, and prayer at home or school or coffee shop — or for reading, practice, and prayer out in nature.

Nature as Spiritual Practice and the *Field Guide* are intended to be read and practiced together, and they are integrated in a way that makes this possible. The intentional placement of practices will broaden and enhance understanding of discussion in the text, while textual reflection will, in a circular way, deepen the impact of your experience of the practice.

You will want to find your own schedule and pace for doing the practices, and for moving between text and practice. *Nature as Spiritual Practice* can be read straight through as any "regular" book; or you can open it to what interests you and read it in parts. Many of the practices are valuable as reading material even if you do not immediately put them into practice. The reason for this is, I think, twofold: (1) Your creative imagination is a valuable resource for experiencing nature as practice; often as you read through a practice, you will creatively imagine doing the practice, which in itself will be informative, formative, and experiential. (2) Your memory is also a valuable resource for experiencing nature as practice. Often you can read through a practice that you do not have the time to do right away, or one where you know of a particular location you would like to do the practice at a later date. Later, when you do the practice, memory of the earlier reading will enhance your experience. Furthermore, many times you will find that, as you explore the natural world, you will remember the practice you have done in the past or have only read, and you may wish to repeat the practice or portions of it even if you do not have the description of the practice with you. Or, even more serendipitously, in the midst of your time in nature you may suddenly realize that you are in fact doing the practice!

Speaking of serendipity, always allow yourself to be playful with the practices. Assimilate the intention and the details of the practice, follow them, then allow your attention and wonder to be guided by creation herself. The *Field Guide* is intended to be taken with you into the "field," referred to as needed, and then, as with any good "field guide," essentially forgotten as attention, wonder, and contemplation of nature themselves capture and begin to guide you. It is my hope that your *Field Guide* will become ragged, torn, dirt-smudged, and berry- or bug-stained over time, as you carry it into the field, alternately leafing through it and meditating on it, pocketing it and dropping it, and taking it home for another day. I often fall asleep while reading my field guides to medicinal plants, wildflowers, and trees.

Some practices are intended to be done only once, others over the course of some days or weeks or months, still others over a lifetime. But again, every practice is itself simply a point of entry to be followed only to the point where nature herself begins to guide you. You will want to work through some of the practices systematically; others will be more "organic" in structure. But when you notice that Something Else is guiding you, make it a practice to follow it.

The practices are also flexible with regard to personal or group use. Regardless of how they are described, most of the practices can be adapted for personal use, for use in small groups, or for use in retreats focused on nature. A sample retreat is given at the end of the practices in this *Field Guide.*

On Journaling, Photography, Art, Canoeing, Hiking, Identifying

All of us have our own ways of seeing, attending to, and being astonished by nature. One way of thinking about how you can see nature more clearly is to think about a phrase used by Gerald May. May writes that there is something within nature that evokes "the power of the slowing." By this he means that, if we give careful attention to nature, it has the ability to slow us down to its pace. (On the other hand, unless manipulated by humans, nature is singularly reluctant to convenience us by stepping up to our pace.) What will help you enter this power of the slowing in nature? Ask yourself what slows you down, what helps you to pay attention, what cultivates a contemplative form of listening and seeing and hearing and responding? For some, journaling is a powerful way to pay careful attention to nature and also provides a record of nature experiences and practices. For others, photography works in much the same way, using different powers of the senses, mind, and concentration. Still others find that canoeing or hiking develops the power of the slowing. Drawing helps others, while still others are brought into the power of the slowing by gardening or by bird watching or using a field guide to identify wildflowers or trees. Different forms of prayer, meditation, and contemplation in nature slow us down to the pace and rhythms of nature. You may find that chopping wood or watching rain brings on the power of the slowing. There are many, many possibilities.

Since there are so many possibilities and so many personalities, my suggestion of journaling in *Nature as Spiritual Practice* and in the *Field Guide* is a kind of a code that invites you to do any of the many possible things that help you most easily enter the power of the slowing.

Using the *Field Guide* for Personal Practice

Depending on your own personality, needs, interests, "smarts" (see below), and desires at this time in your life, you can read the book organically or systematically. You may choose to read a section or do a practice as they attract you for whatever reason (organically), or you may choose to read through a chapter or set of sections from beginning to end, taking time to do the practices as they are arranged (systematically). You will probably find that some combination of these two approaches is most helpful. With text or practice, you may initially pick several practices and do them over time, returning to the text as you feel the need; or you may expand one exercise over the duration of a few days or weeks or months. However you proceed, you will soon become aware that, though your experience may be personal, it is never personal in the sense of being individual or isolated: creation practice teaches that personal identity formation is also always formation in community.

It is also important to speak aloud your formational encounter with creation. Sharing what we learn and experience in nature is often difficult since we have neglected the spiritual arts of these connective practices in nature for so long. But in sharing and verbalizing your journey, you will begin to experience the heartbeat of nature as a vast web of connection. Ideally, you will have a friend, pastor, spiritual director, spouse, or group with whom you can begin exploring how to communicate and refine your kinship with nature. You may wish to begin each exercise acknowledging your desire to grow in connection with nature, yourself, others, and God. This can be done in prayer, or through some ritual, or a simple acknowledgment of your intention before God.

Spiritual practice in nature changes and transforms mind and body and soul. It is not the practice that instigates change and transformation; it is the spirit of Christ working through creation. The organic reality of nature disassembles even our best intentions. So the "intention" of this book is really to learn to let go of our intentions and to embrace creation's more dynamic, organic ways of being.

Finally, in your own way, know and believe that the divine is accompanying you on this journey of formation and discovery.

Using the Practices with Multiple Ways of Learning

Each of the practices in this book is intended to be very flexible, especially with respect to the different ways of learning that are unique to each person. The now widely accepted theory of multiple intelligences, developed in 1983 by Howard Gardner, a professor of education at Harvard University, came about largely as a result of his dissatisfaction with the standard IQ tests that measure only certain ways of knowing or learning. Gardner instead proposed seven types of learning or intelligences to account for the broader range of human ways of knowing. The simple and quick evaluation instrument given in Appendix B in *Nature as Spiritual Practice* will help you assess the two or three intelligence types (or "smarts") that best describe how you learn and understand the world around you. As you work through the practices, allow your own particular ways of processing information to guide you in following the practices as given or adapting them in ways that are better suited to your own "smarts."[3]

Since nature is accessed in so many ways, it is not surprising that since his earlier work, Gardner has suggested an eighth intelligence: "nature smart" (naturalist intelligence). Work in this type of intelligence has just begun, but Professor Leslie Owen Wilson at the University of Wisconsin has developed a list of descriptors for this eighth kind of intelligence.[4] Wilson finds that people who are "nature smart" have keen sensory skills, including sight, sound, smell, taste, and touch, that help them to notice and categorize things from the natural world. They like outside activities like gardening, nature walks, or field trips geared toward observing nature or natural phenomenon and easily notice patterns from their surroundings — differences, similarities, anomalies. People who are "nature smart" notice things in the environment that others often miss. Such people show heightened awareness of and concern for the environment and endangered species, and easily learn characteristics, names, categorizations, and data about objects or species found in the natural world.

The practices in this book are intended to exercise our "nature smarts" in ways that contribute to Christian identity formation. Once again, be creative with your practice and your time in nature! Allow your own "multiple intelligences" to interact with your growing "nature smarts" in ways that serve to reconnect you with the entirety of creation.

Using the *Field Guide* in Group Settings or Retreats

Meaning in the natural world is often found in solitude. Meaning in the natural world is also often found in community, which is not surprising given creation's own intricate communal webs of meaning. The gentle movement between solitude and community is a foundational lesson of creation: transition, as nature teaches, is a practice. The practices in this book can and should be exercised in solitude and as a part of a community or group as needed. Practices can be adapted to either personal explorations or group settings. Whether entirely personal, initially personal with

3. "Nature smarts" was not included in the original seven types of intelligences and thus is not a part of the inventory in Appendix B.

4. The descriptors are listed in Richard Louv, *The Last Child in the Woods: Saving Our Children from Nature-Deficit Disorder* (Chapel Hill, NC: Algonquin Books, 2005), 72-73. Chapter 6 in Louv's book (pp. 70-84) is devoted to this eighth intelligence.

later "processing" in small groups, or practiced and processed in community, the practices can be formed to fit the needs of church or parish education and formation, academic courses, or personal or group retreats. The material is intended for the laity, pastors, priests, and religious educators, as well as undergraduate, seminary, or graduate courses, or anyone with an awakening sense of the mystery and pattern of creation. Regardless of the recipient, the gifts of nature will also inevitably raise awareness of and commitment to creation care, ecological restoration, and lifestyles that honor and sustain creation resources. For retreats — personal or group — the practices can be grouped in any number of ways that will help focus and deepen the broader intention of the retreat. A sample retreat is given at the end of this *Field Guide*. Additional suggestions for using the practices in a retreat setting are given in that sample retreat.

If you are facilitating a retreat or using practices in a group, identify the relative need for use of text (theory) and practice (experience) that is most appropriate for your group. Take some time to think about "learner outcomes," but do not be tied to these. Nature is one place where agendas and "learner outcomes" are entirely unpredictable. Also, if you are leading the group, be familiar with the details of the practice so that you can explain them clearly to participants. It will be most helpful for each participant to have the *Field Guide to Nature as Spiritual Practice* to refer to during any given practice and *Nature as Spiritual Practice* as a tool to help participants begin to think about the implications of their experience in nature. It is often helpful to gather in a circle beforehand to read the complete practice, to let everyone know the time frame for a particular practice, and to pray. If your group is covenanting to explore creation practice or formation over time, offer one or two practices to be done between meetings and discuss participants' experience of these at the next gathering. Whatever the structure of your group, it is important to find a balance between opportunities to spend time in solitude in nature, opportunities to move from experiences of solitude to processing of those experiences with others, and opportunities to reflect on the experiences by reading and discussing *Nature as Spiritual Practice.*

For processing practices: (1) ensure that each participant can commit to the entire process to allow sufficient trust to be built; (2) allow all to contribute actively, but maintain boundaries that are appropriate and safe; (3) allow all group members to share equally in discussion or processing; (4) do not offer advice or try to "fix" another's perspective or ideas; and (5) maintain strict group confidentiality.

Most important of all in the dynamics of doing and processing spiritual practice in groups is the art of contemplative listening. Listening is essential both in nature and when gathered together in a group. What Elizabeth Liebert writes on contemplative listening in groups can also be applied to contemplative "listening" to creation: "Contemplative listening seeks to honor the presence of the Holy Spirit in the speaker and between listener and speaker. Such listening rests in warm, loving, engaged, and prayerful silence, which often needs few or no words."[5] You will find that creation, too, has much to teach you about listening.

In groups, contemplative listening also includes contemplative response. A few common modes of contemplative response in groups include phrases such as:

"I heard you say . . . [repeat, in same or similar words, what you heard]."
"It seems that you . . . [repeat what speaker did or felt] because . . . [name the expression, action, or tone of voice that supports your educated guess]."
"I noticed that you . . . [describe something the person said or did, but without interpreting it]."
"There seems to be a pattern . . . [briefly describe the two or three aspects that link together]."

Finally, with any practice or retreat, factor in time for "wandering" or rest with no agenda at all. Nature will provide one! And the most important thing to remember in using this material is to turn your hunger for a deepening relationship with God . . . toward nature. In doing so, you will find that creation shares exactly the same hunger.

5. Elizabeth Liebert, *The Way of Discernment: Spiritual Practices for Decision Making* (Louisville: Westminster John Knox, 2008), xix. Liebert's introduction contains an excellent section on participating in and leading retreats.

Practices from *Nature as Spiritual Practice*

The practices that follow include those given in full in the text as well as the complete practice for those for which only the "title" and "intention" are given in *Nature as Spiritual Practice*. The arrangement of practices in *Nature as Spiritual Practice* is intended to permit maximum integration between experience (practice) and critical reflection (text). For easy cross-referencing, the practices below are keyed numerically to the chapter in which they are first introduced in *Nature as Spiritual Practice*.

On Earth as It Is

CHAPTER ONE

"Thy Will Be Done, on Earth as It Is . . ."

PRACTICE 1.1

Ah!

[Full practice also in *Nature as Spiritual Practice*]

INTENTION   The intention of this practice is to begin to notice and respond to nature "on earth as it is."

PRACTICE   The theologian Dorothée Sölle identifies five possible "responses on seeing a flower":

> Ah!
> Oh, beautiful — I want it, but I will let it be!
> Oh, beautiful — I want it, I will take it!
> Oh, beautiful — I can sell it!
> So?[1]

- Find something in the natural world that captures your attention or recall your past experiences. Reflect honestly on how you respond to this object: in other words, how do you "respond on seeing a flower"?
- The following are key concepts developed in this and the chapters that follow. How, at this time, do each of the following affect your possible responses to nature?
  - No part of creation is left void of the Word of God.
  - There is no place we can learn but from the place itself.

1. Dorothée Sölle, *Christianity and Crisis*, quoted in Nancy Roth, *Organic Prayer: A Spiritual Gardening Companion* (New York: Seabury Books, 2007), 114.

- Creation is both seen (ecological and material) and unseen (sacramental and relational).
- Every creature knows its Creator and reaches back to the Lord.
- If we listen, we find that nature has its own way of speaking.
- We are accustomed to separating nature and human perception into two realms; they are, in fact, indivisible.
- Today the earth is suffering.
- At the same time that the earth is suffering, it still provides healing, solace, and guidance.
- Christ is not here (within the tomb where he was laid) because he is now everywhere.

• How would you *like* to respond to creation — "on earth as it is"?

PRACTICE 1.2

God Resides in Places: Attention as Contemplative Prayer

INTENTION   We have learned that God is simultaneously transcendent (beyond all things) and immanent (known through all things). This practice focuses on the immanent nature of the divine, with the intention of assimilating the phrase "God resides in places" on an experiential level and to allow the experience to become prayer.

PRACTICE   The best way to do this practice is in a location in the natural world where you, quite spontaneously, experience nature in a very strong way. The place may be one that brings joy, longing, and desire, or a rush of feelings of gratitude, a sense of overwhelming beauty, a sense of peace through stillness and silence, or a location that gives relief to some worry or mourning or sadness. You will know such a place when you find it. In fact, it will be finding you! It will call you. You may experience this as God's call, but don't worry if you have no "sense" of God's presence at this time. Simply allow the attention, the connection, the place to become prayer for you.

• Whether sitting, walking, or standing, take careful note of your own feelings as you enter, explore, and settle into this place. Note the physical or material characteristics of the place — space and time — around you and how you feel connected to them.
• Breathe simply and in rhythm for a time to clear your consciousness of distraction.

- Then begin by performing this simple exercise: touch objects, shapes, and surfaces of anything around you in nature that you would like. Each time you touch something, say a simple silent (or internal) "thank you" or let it "speak" to you. Then begin doing the same for things you see: say a simple silent "thank you." Experiment by doing the same with all your senses: smell, taste, and hear with a simple "thank you." Give thanks for any thoughts or feelings you become aware of.
- As you are ready, let your presence and the natural world around you become prayer based on your contemplative attention and senses. Notice how this is prayer: it could be an internal conversation, or recollection, or lament; perhaps you sense your prayer as relationship, sacred or ecological; your prayer can also be one of simple presence and connection; your focused attention or a capacity for wonder is likewise contemplative prayer.
- Before you leave your place, notice your breathing and what your breath adds to prayer and what your breath tells you about your connection to creation around you. All plants and animals are breathing in rhythm around you.
- As you leave, carry your prayer with you: you are already carrying your breath and you are already carrying your body, both of which were/are a part of your prayer. Also carry your attention, your wonder, your memory as you move into new places as new possibilities for prayer.

PRACTICE 1.3

Consolation, Grief, and Loss
[Full practice also in *Nature as Spiritual Practice*]

INTENTION The intention of this practice is to recover in your memory places in nature you have gone for consolation and to return there or find new places in the natural world that comfort you.

PRACTICE There are two aspects of this practice that are important to notice: (1) where you go when you feel pain, suffering, or loss; (2) noticing what about nature has the ability to "consume" grief, bringing comfort, calm, equilibrium, and peace.

- Recall places or a place in nature where in the past you have gone when you were feeling sadness or grief. If you can't think of a particular place, recall the last few times you were sad, then think back, remembering places you went during that time.

- As you look back, is there a particular landscape or part of creation that comforts you during times of grief and loss? What is the most consoling environment you have experienced?
- What is it about a particular place that attracts you when you are sad, in mourning, or hurting? Simply recall places you have been with nature in sadness. Recall what you were doing at the time: walking, sitting, running, writing, kayaking, crying, photographing. Again, what part of your grief was absorbed by this place in nature?
- If you can, return to this place if it is near. What does it feel like to you now, and what do you notice about it?
- We all suffer grief or loss, more so at certain periods of our lives, less at other times. Consciously seek a place in nature that soothes and comforts you. You may find yourself on a bench in a city park, or aggressively chopping wood, or gathering blackberries, or sitting on a beach.
- Notice how nature "sits" with you as it consoles and comforts. How is nature an active partner in consolation? Nature may calm; it may help put into perspective a particular sorrow; its very "isness," or presence, may redirect sorrow in a healing direction. Let yourself absorb this healing. How did — or does — nature bring solace? How would you describe or communicate it?
- How can you be present to another person in the way nature has been present to you in sorrow? How can you be present to nature in the same way?

PRACTICE 1.4

The Fertility of Silence

See your prayer as arousing the letters
through which heaven and earth
and all living things were created.
The letters are the life of all;
when you pray through them,
all Creation joins with you in prayer.
All that is around you can be uplifted;

even the song of a passing bird
may enter into such a prayer.

INTENTION   One of the beautiful antiphons of Lent is: "May the fertility of silence give life and power to our words and deeds — Lord, give us hope." I have suggested that creation is a kind of "visible hope" that emerges and is sustained by God out of what we might call a "fertility of silence." In this practice we meditate on what it might be like if this were not the case.

PRACTICE   Find a spot in creation that calls and attracts you, a place where you will not be disturbed and where you can give your full attention to nature, God, and yourself. You can focus on an ecological system defined by the outer limits of all your senses or on a single object, such as a shell or a dragonfly. Bring the short Hasidic meditation given above along with you, and read and meditate on it before and/or during the practice.

- For this practice it will be important to attend to all that you possibly can about the place or the object. This includes everything that you can take in through your senses, all you see, feel, hear, smell, taste — everything you can notice about the place or object, from color and weight to how it aligns itself and moves or is stationary in space, to how it marks the time. Use your imagination, intellect, memory, intuition, will, and love. Notice not only the "exterior" object or place, but also how you are feeling "inside." You are in effect giving yourself sabbatical time to watch and notice and to be in relationship with creation.
- Such noticing and such relationships are, as the Hasidic teachers remind us, prayer.
- When you are ready, slowly begin to "strip away" — one at a time — the characteristics and attributes from the system or thing you have been noticing: if you have been sitting on a beach at the ocean, imagine that there is no sound of waves, then no sound of birds, wind, or hearing itself. Strip away each color one by one and all else you see. Strip away memories that the beach or ocean evoke. Strip away everything you can possibly imagine that connects you to nature. Let all these collapse into nothing.
- Now strip away imagination itself, and then connection. Give yourself time. When you have moved to stripping away imagination, then connection, stay with the practice for another fifteen to twenty minutes: nature has no recognizable attributes. In the silence, it is natural that

thoughts, images, or deeper realities of nature will continue periodically to arise in your awareness. As you notice these, simply let them go. As this occurs, it may be helpful to focus briefly on your breath or gently to "cover" the thought with a single word, such as "love" or "God."

- At the end of your time, allow yourself a few moments to reclaim the fertility of silence.
- Give yourself a few minutes to readjust to your normal ways of being conscious in the world.
- As you prepare to leave, slowly and contemplatively notice once again those things that you "stripped away" earlier. Notice how you experience the world around you now. Notice God's absence or presence.
- Pray the Lenten antiphon: "May the fertility of silence give life and power to our words and deeds — Lord, give us hope."

PRACTICE 1.5

God Was Pleased

[Full practice also in *Nature as Spiritual Practice*]

> Do you not say, "Four months more, then comes the harvest"? But I tell you, look around you, and see how the fields are ripe for harvesting.
>
> John 4:35

INTENTION Scripture and nature tell God's story, one to the other. In this passage from John, Jesus sees all things two ways, simultaneously: he sees both what is and what will be. He sees "ripeness" now, and he sees the "ripeness" of the harvest time. Notice that Christ communicates this "double vision" via a story that includes nature and her seasons. In fact, this "double vision" is possible only through a reciprocating attention between the book of nature and the book of Scripture. As an example of "double vision" made possible by the intersection between Scripture and nature, the intention of this practice is to participate in Jesus' own "double-sighted" vision of creation.

PRACTICE Meditate on the above passage from John 4. Notice that, though Jesus recognizes that the harvest will arrive in four months, he also sees that in some important way these same fields are already ripe for harvesting now!

- Walk into the natural world into a place that attracts you. Spend time there noting the season, noting when leaves may fall or berries may become ripe or the first snow may fall — sometime in the future. In doing so, you are a human engaged in the cycles of creation. In exactly the same way, Christ was a human engaged in the cycles of the seasons.
- Now take a closer look around you. What is "ripe for harvesting" now? One way to put this metaphor plainly is: What do you experience as sacred (ripe) now? How can you be present, as was Jesus, to creation in both her ecological and sacramental realities? It might help to recall Moses' experience with the burning bush: it was on fire, yet the bush was not consumed. The bush remained precisely what it was ecologically even as it raged with a fire of the sacred. Practice experiencing nature in this way. It may also help, as it did for Moses, to remove your shoes.
- Again, Jesus sees the time of natural harvesting in four months at the same time that he points out the sacred harvest of the field here and now. Practice joining Jesus in this "dual vision" of creation.
- How do the "double stories" of Scripture and creation help complete this vision?

CHAPTER TWO

Definitions and Intentions

PRACTICE 2.1

Finding a Place Not Sacred?

INTENTION   One of the real disagreements in discussions about "nature," "earth," and "creation" is about what is sacred in these places and what is not. This practice involves a few simple imaginary games: (1) to suggest that we can, in fact, choose to find the sacred in nature; (2) to suggest that from a certain perspective, through attentiveness or awareness, it is possible to recognize that any created place is sacred; and (3) to suggest that an "ordinary" place is "ordinary" only because we participate in it in an "ordinary" way.

PRACTICE

- Imagine or remember a time when creation did not choose you but you chose it. What were the qualities of the place that made you "choose" to give attention?
- Now simply wander in nature and purposefully settle in to a place that really doesn't appeal to you much — at least initially. Wait in this place, give it your careful attention, then notice a few subjects within this place that evoke curiosity or wonder. Or just notice how the place helps you lose yourself for a moment in peace.
- Notice as you do this that, in waiting and giving attention, you are finding your own way to ritualize a seemingly ordinary place. That is, simply waiting or being in nature is itself a kind of ritual. You are participating in movement, stability, shapes, symbols, physicality, and spirituality,

all of which and more combine to give meaning to place through ritual. In defining ritual, nature is giving shape to the sacred. This is not at all obscure or fanciful. Imagine, for instance, what roles you might play in a marriage ceremony and the symbols that characterize the ceremony as sacred ritual: bride, groom, bride's maid, father of the bride, mother of the groom, pastor, priest, family, friends, casual onlookers, music, walking, words, ring, flowers, gowns, dresses, colors, kisses, hopes and dreams. Now resume giving attention to nature as you would give attention and participate in a wedding ceremony. Attention and the ceremony unite in ritual while the constant ritual of nature unites participants in a kind of "kiss." What is ecological about this "kiss"? What is sacramental about this ritualizing kiss of creation?

- Another way to enter into the sacred or participate with nature is to acknowledge that you and this place of creation are of common parentage.
- How is this place in nature similar to Scripture in the way it draws you toward God? How is it different? As you reflect, imagine another "ordinary" place in nature.
- Can you imagine any "ordinary" place that, approached through a prayerful ritual of attention and wonder, is not "sacred"?
- As you leave, acknowledge this place's common parentage to you through a small ritual or prayer of your own.

PRACTICE 2.2

Ecosystem Game

INTENTION Arthur Tansley writes that ecological systems "are not only included as parts of larger ones, but they also overlap, interlock and interact with one another." Using a group ecosystem game, the intent of this practice is to experience ecology as an interdependent, self-organizing, internally motivated, and interlocking system.

PRACTICE Two practices are suggested: one to be done as a group, another that can be done in solitude. The practices allow participants to experience in an embodied way the interdependent, self-organizing, and internally motivated quality of ecosystems.

Group Ecosystem Game:
- Preferably outside, have each participant choose two other people in the group, without in any way indicating whom they choose.

- When the game starts (with bell or other signal), the group begins to move and all participants try to keep an equal distance between the two (anonymous) members they have chosen.
- As the group moves, the activity will speed up and slow down at various times; it may almost stop, but it will restart again. Give it at least five minutes.
- At the end of five minutes, ask the group the following questions:

  1. What did you experience?
  2. Was it apparent who, if anyone, was keeping a distance from you?
  3. What did you use as feedback to do this game? Could you have done it with your eyes closed?

- Have two or three people, randomly picked, now remain stationary. This time have each member choose one additional group member anonymously. Have the group begin to move now in the same way, keeping equal distance between the two or three stationary members (who are known by all). At the end of a few minutes ask the following:

  1. What did you experience this time? Was it the same or different?
  2. Did you experience any dysfunction in the system?
  3. Would anyone care to or be able to volunteer to organize this movement?
  4. What does this tell you about God's role in ecosystems?

Personal Practice:
- Find a place where you can sit and watch the natural world. Spend as much time as you can, as carefully as you can, attending to the environment around you. As you notice each new object or group of objects, ask yourself how they are connected to other elements of this ecosystem. How is the system you notice self-regulating, that is, how does it maintain its own systemic, organic structure? As an interlocking yet open system, on what does it depend that comes from outside of itself for its survival?
- As you are ready, choose an easily identifiable object that marks and identifies the place: it may be a tree, a large rock, a grouping of bushes, or even a circle you construct of stones.
- Wander away from this place slowly. Pay attention to what you see around you. The second chapter in Gerald G. May's book *The Wisdom of Wilderness* may be a helpful aid: it is called "The Power of the Slowing."

Wander, under the power of nature's slowing, but in such a way that you eventually return to your starting point and your identifying marker.

- How is the place/marker the same? How has it changed? You are the same person, and yet in many ways you have altered: you perceive the familiar in new ways. From any starting place, or "home," the transitions from leaving and returning are as important as the journey of wandering or the home. We bring something of our home along with us on our journeys, just as we bring something of our wandering home.
- How are these wanderings, "homes," and rhythms similar to and different from your relationship with God?

PRACTICE 2.3

Attention as Contemplative Reawakening[1]
[Full Practice also in *Nature as Spiritual Practice*]

INTENTION   People become animated talking about even brief connections with nature. The intention of this practice is — "intentionally" — to awaken us from perceptual sleepiness to an awareness (contemplation) of our place in nature and to our habitual connection to it.

PRACTICE   Our awareness is shaped by what we choose to pay attention to. When we focus our attention primarily on human-made things and activities, our consciousness of creation naturally diminishes. In fact, consciousness itself diminishes.

- Identify an object or location in nature that attracts your attention. This could be as close as your own backyard, a nearby park, a tree outside your bedroom window, a bird singing at sunrise — any thing or place that "speaks" to you.
- Illuminate or "shine" your awareness on this object or location. Illuminate it with your senses by looking, listening, smelling, touching. As you are ready, "shine" your memory and imagination and intuition on this object or location. In other words, consume this location to the utmost of your attentive powers.

1. This practice is given in part in Philip Sutton Chard, *The Healing Earth: Nature's Medicine for the Troubled Soul* (Minnetonka, MN: NorthWord Press, 1994), 37.

- For several consecutive days, return to study this same object or place, and each time seek to notice some other aspect of it that previously escaped your attention.
- Pay attention to the tremendous variations and subtleties of the relationship that form over time. You might wish to go to a place in nature during different times of the year, taking photographs of the same scene each time. Noticing the changes over time in this way can sometimes be startling. A lake or river can awaken you in new ways no matter how many times you visit it. On the other hand, be prepared for the fact that at times, even with your senses open, you will sense nothing new, numinous, or even — perhaps at times — anything very interesting at all. At other times, moments that you share with nature with a purely open and wandering mind can be refreshing in themselves. At still other times, you will find yourself enfolded in sacred matters.
- To be honest, at times nature will simply bore you. Boredom is a part of a relationship. Talk with nature about being bored!
- Over time, and as you are taken by nature and nature by you, you will find that nature opens your senses and enlivens your soul. Creation becomes a kind of gift, an offering prepared by God for awakening and illuminating our bodies and minds and spirits.

PRACTICE 2.4

De-Creating Genesis

INTENTION The intention of this practice is to experience creation, not as transferred, imagistic, or symbolic, but as ecological (material) and sacramental (spiritual) reality. We will do this by using the first Genesis creation story, reading it in reverse. Two phases of meditation are used for each day, starting from the seventh day: (1) we first enter guided meditation on what was created on this day as described in Genesis; (2) we then move through guided meditation, imagining that God did not, in fact, create that day or any of its creations. The guided meditation takes us back to the time before God "began" creation. The intention of the practice is this: in stripping creation of all we "imagine" it to be, we will see it as it is, as pure doxology.

PRACTICE This practice can be done indoors, solely through the imagination; but it is more effective to do outside in nature. This practice works best guided by a facilitator (usually with a group), who takes participants slowly through each day. It can also be done alone, also preferably in nature. Whether with a facilitator or reading through it on your own, allow ample time to imagine and/or notice the things of creation as they are named and ample time for meditation between each day as the day and its creations melt away. Participants may lie on their backs on the earth or sit (or even walk if it is a small group and you have more than an hour). This practice may be done entirely as a meditation with eyes closed, or with eyes and ears open, or as a more tactile practice in which you notice, experience, and interact with elements of creation as they are described. I have described this practice assuming this more active, tactile approach; but it is just as effective as a guided meditation. With a facilitator or on your own, as you progress back through the creation days, the only change in the order of the creation story is that you will imagine humanity to have been created first. This will be done so that you, as a human, can stay with the practice to the end. Toward the end of the meditation, then, you will also imagine that God did not create humanity.

- Pick a place in nature where you will not be interrupted.
- Settle in and relax. Sit or lie on your back, close your eyes, and follow the guided imagination as it unfolds.
- On the seventh day (Gen. 2:1-3), with the "heavens and the earth completed," God rests. God blesses this seventh day and makes it holy. Rest in all that God has done in creation. Close your eyes. Rest. Receive God's blessing on the day, and accept the holiness of where and what you are. Take pleasure in all God has created. Know that it is good. Rest in this creation made of love. Notice the wind and your breath, and feel the earth beneath you. Recite to yourself: "Be still and know that I am God." "Be still and know that I am." "Be still and know." "Be still." "Be."
- On the sixth day (Gen. 1:26-27), God created humankind, man and woman, in God's own image and likeness. You are God's image and likeness. Notice how it feels to be God's image and likeness. "God saw everything God made, and indeed it was very good" (Gen. 1:31). Know that God is speaking to you; indeed, you are very good. As though for the first time, having just been created, briefly open your eyes on this newly created world, a world that is blessed, good, and holy. Close your eyes, knowing again that you and all creation around you are indeed all very good.

- With you and the rest of humanity, also on the sixth day (Gen. 1:24-25), God speaks and the earth brings forth living creatures of every kind: cattle of every kind and creeping things of every kind and wild animals of every kind. See if you can find just one: an insect is good. Notice all you can about your "creeping thing." See that it is good and blessed. Then imagine that this portion of the sixth day did not take place. Imagine that there is no other humanity besides yourself, no wild or tame or "creeping things" on the earth. Your insect is gone from the face of the earth. Notice that this good, this blessing, is no more.

- On the fifth day (Gen. 1:20-23), God speaks the waters into bringing forth within them swarms of living creatures and great sea monsters, and speaks the skies into producing birds that fly above the earth. Find a fish or sea mammal or, more likely, a bird. Spend some time with this living thing, seeing that it is good and blessed. Marvel at its beauteous and creative existence. Then imagine that this fifth day did not take place and that this particular living creature — in fact, every living creature that flies and every creature in the seas — is no more.

- On the fourth day (Gen. 1:14-19), God speaks and separates the night from the day by placing the sun to rule the day and the moon the night, creating times and seasons. God sets stars in the dome of the night. These are signs for seasons and for days and years. Take some time to be with the ruler of the day or the night. Watch and experience for a while as the light shifts and changes, as the shadows move with the movement of the sun or moon. Notice all you can about the day, the year, the season. See how blessed and good are the sun and moon and stars, the days and years and seasons. Now imagine that there was no fourth day. Light is still separate from the dark, but there is no moon, no sun, no stars, no galaxies. There are no years, no seasons. These goods and blessings are no more. Light and dark yet remain, having been created on the first day; but there is no sun. Notice how you are feeling. Plants and earth and waters and light and dark remain, and time remains — but without sun and seasons, only as a single day. This is all that remains of time. Notice what is happening to nature. Notice how you feel about God.

- On the third day (Gen. 1:9-13), God speaks many things into being. God gathers the waters together, dry land appears, and the dry land brings forth vegetation of every kind. "Earth" itself is named, and earth puts forth plants yielding seed and fruit trees of every kind. Feel the earth as it "supports" you in every sense of the word. You spend most of your life on this dry land, yet the seas are there also in their vastness. Pick out a plant or a tree or a bush or group of flowers nearby and notice all you can about them, how they add to the beauty around you. See how blessed and good are the earth, the seas, all plants and flowers, all seeds and fruit. Now, slowly imagine all these things dissolving as if the third day had never occurred. Imagine all plants and vegetation, trees, forests, fruits, vines, grass, and all things yielding seed as though they never existed. Imagine that all dry land is gone. Imagine that all seas are gone. You are now floating on the face of the waters.

- On the second day (Gen. 1:6-8), God speaks and creates expanse, literally creates space itself to separate the waters from the waters. This first expanse or first space God calls "sky." Lie on your back (you will have to imagine doing so on water, because there is no land), gaze up into the sky, and notice all you can about the sky. Linger on space. What is space? Space itself is created, and it is blessed and good. As you are ready, imagine that the sky is no more. Now, slowly imagine that space is no more. There is no "separation between" waters: waters still cover the face of the earth, but there is no dimension, no length, height, width, or breadth. How do you orient yourself? Without space, what are you? Time remains as a single day, but not space. You are floating on a face of water with no sky, no earth, no up, no down, only darkness and light.

- On the first day (Gen. 1:3-5), God creates light and separates it from the darkness. Light is the hope of the world. There is something called "day" and something called "night," the first sense of time, the first light. Light is blessed and light is good. Experience the light where you are and imagine all the things that light warms, illuminates, encourages, penetrates, and sustains. Now imagine that there is no light. There is only darkness. How do you experience "no light"? What is "darkness" where there is no light? The good and the blessing of light is no more. Stay with the practice.

- Before the creation there was "beginning": so something in relationship to "time," something named "beginning," existed. Before "beginning" there is no time. There is only formless void: it is chaos (in Hebrew, *tohu bohu).* We have a kind of "darkness" that is without light. There is no time. Nothing is said of goodness or blessing, because this *tohu bohu,* this darkness and chaos, is not good. Enter the "face of the deep"; drop into *tohu bohu;* become a formless void; you are gone. All is not. All is gone.

- Close your eyes on a "time" before the beginning: there are no heavens, no earth, no formlessness, no chaos, not even darkness, no "singularity." No words. Meditate on this phrase: "imagination dead imagine."
- Let go of all consciousness.
- God is uncreated. Where and what are you? Even "dead" is no more.
- Stay with this as long as you are able to. Explore the singularity of a Creator without a creation.
- When you need to "return," come back slowly. Allow yourself to become present once again "on earth as it is." Notice how you are feeling, what you are thinking. Notice any changes or transformations in your connection to God, nature, yourself, and others.
- Take time to thank God for everything created as they slowly come back to your attention. Acknowledge in your own way that all creation is good, blessed, and holy. What is creation to you now? How do you pay attention to it? Has your experience diminished or increased wonder? How do you experience creation as praise?
- End by reading the following from the Song of Songs:

> A garden locked is my sister, my bride,
>   a garden locked, a fountain sealed. . . .
> Awake, O north wind,
>   and come, O south wind!
> Blow upon my garden
>   that its fragrance may be wafted abroad.
>
> Song of Songs 4:12, 16

Sacramental Ecology

CHAPTER THREE

The Sacred Matters

The Sacred Matters
[Full practice also in *Nature as Spiritual Practice*]

INTENTION Acknowledging that the sacred matters.

PRACTICE In this practice, be astonished by nature as you are called to do so, or simply be with nature in a more detached but open way.

- Explore the physical and spiritual characteristics of nature. Notice what and how nature incorporates your attention and wonder: possibilities are as diverse as a rock or the wind or how sunlight strikes the ground or how the fish are biting or how you experience some interconnected features of nature. It will involve using all your perceptions, thoughts, memories, intuitions, feelings, imaginings, creativity, hopes, dreams, faith, body, soul, and love. You can attend to nature in ways that appeal to you: through journaling, photography, drawing, or using a field guide to focus in on particular features of nature.
- Explore what captures your attention in its material nature.
- Similarly, explore how nature offers you its sacred aspect.
- Notice the here and now, the how, where, and when of material nature, then whether and/or how this same material nature takes on sacred qualities.
- Similarly, notice the here and now, the how, where, and when of sacred nature as it is or becomes material.

31

- How do the material and the spiritual (the ecological and the sacramental) mutually enhance one another?
- As you experience this, is one possible without the other?
- Try to behold the sacred and material in balance. As they move out of balance, as they inevitably will (for instance, you begin to notice only the sound of a cedar waxwing as sound, or as one series of notes in a sacred creation-symphony of bird song), be attentive to the shift. Can you control the shift? Notice what you experience as balance between sacred and matter in nature over time.
- Practice this form of contemplative attention (by yourself and in nature) at random times. How does your sensitivity to the material and the spiritual qualities of nature evolve?

PRACTICE 3.2

An Ecological Perception of Place[1]

INTENTION   One of the best ways to awaken wonder and attentiveness to nature is to know your environment. The intention of this practice is just that: to get to know your local environment more thoroughly in all its variety and specificity. As you do so, you will notice its beauty. You will also notice some other things: how nature is being degraded by human actions, and also how — in nature — violence, death, and renewal must become a part of your attention and wonder.

PRACTICE   If you are not already a specialist in some aspect of your environment/ecology, the two suggestions below will awaken both attention and wonder, give you pleasure over time, and ensure that you get into nature and explore it in a consistent way. (If you are already a specialist, so much the better!) This is a practice for which you will need to do some research on your own. But the research itself will be rewarding and will increase your capacity to notice, attend to, and interact with the natural world in creative and caring ways.

---

1. This phrase is suggested in Steven Bouma-Prediger, *For the Beauty of the Earth: A Christian Vision for Creation Care* (Grand Rapids: Baker Academic, 2001). His first chapter (pp. 19-38) is especially good at providing suggestions for developing such an "ecological perception of place."

- Form an ecological perception of place. That is, get to know your ecology by becoming familiar over time with as many components of your ecology as you can. For instance, what is the soil like around your home? What are five agricultural plants in your area? How long is the growing season? What geological events or processes have influenced the geography of your region? Name five trees that grow in your area. What birds are common? Which ones are resident and which migratory? What flowers bloom where you live? What animals share your place? When is the moon full in your area, and what constellations appear on a clear night at a given time of year? How does weather arrive in your area? What kinds of clouds accompany what kinds of weather? From which directions does the wind blow? What plants that grow naturally are edible? What plants are medicinal?
- Form an ecological perception of place by getting to know one portion of your ecology well. One of the best ways for you to do this, if you are an "amateur," is to purchase and use a field guide on a subject that interests you. Not only can this become a lifetime hobby (even passion), but in getting to know a particular subject — for instance, wildflowers — you will naturally come to know other components of wildflower ecology as well. Three reliable field guides are the Peterson "field guides," the Smithsonian handbooks, and the National Audubon Society field guides. A sampling of possible subjects include: birds, butterflies, mammals, fishes, fossils, insects and spiders, mammals, mushrooms, night sky, reptiles and amphibians, rocks and minerals, seashells, seashore creatures, trees, weather, and wildflowers.
- Again, the best way to gain these ecological perceptions of place is to research them on your own (or with a group of similar interest) and explore nature to find and identify your favorite ecological niche (again, on your own or with a group with similar interests, such as bird watching). Whatever you choose, you will be amazed at what else you begin to notice about the natural world, especially as nature affects your particular subject — be it birds or wildflowers or trees.

Nature as Praise

INTENTION   The intention of this practice is to begin to notice how nature is in constant praise of God and to join nature in that praise. If this praise awakens "wonder" and "radical amazement" as well, so much the better!

PRACTICE   Scripture is full of descriptions of nature in prayers of thanksgiving and praise to its Creator. Just a few from the book of Psalms include Psalm 19, 66, 96–98, 100, and 148. In the context of this praise, many other passages in Scripture that describe creation's relationship to the Creator imply thanksgiving and praise, for example, Psalm 104.

- Read these psalms and find other passages in Scripture that describe nature in praise.
- Having read these, take a wandering walk in nature and behold how nature gives glory to God simply by being what it is.
- One way of doing this is to approach nature with "wonder" or "radical amazement." You may prefer to think of wonder in this sense as beauty or design.
- With your senses and your imagination open, you will begin to see anything of nature as a gesture of praise to God: movement, color, sensations, stillness, a stone or a white-oak leaf or a redwood forest or a star. Doing any of the following may help you perceive nature as praise:
  - Sink deeply into nature herself.
  - Perform some action on behalf of nature.
  - Allow nature to draw you into a deeper presence with God.
  - Notice new levels of self-understanding.
  - Sense a closer connection with nature.
  - Discover fresh ways of giving attention and wonder to nature.
- Now, how do you experience creation praising God?
- And now, let yourself go: praise God like a wave; praise God like the wind; praise God like a rolling river; praise God like the sun; praise God like an elk.

CHAPTER FOUR

A Covenant with Mystery

Our Covenant with Mystery
[Full practice also in *Nature as Spiritual Practice*]

INTENTION   The intention of this practice is to enter a covenant of mystery with creation.

PRACTICE   The practice entitled "An Ecological Perception of Place" (p. 32, above) will help you focus on nature in ways that will make it easier to enter into a covenant of wonder with nature.

A covenant is an agreement, contract, promise, or pledge. There are two kinds of biblical covenants between God and humanity:[1]

1. Conditional: a covenant that guarantees God will do God's part when *humans meet the requirements* stipulated in that covenant.
2. Unconditional: distinguished from a conditional covenant by the fact that its *ultimate fulfillment* is promised by God and depends on God's power and sovereignty for its fulfillment.

- Allow yourself some time to seek and find an object or ecosystem with which you are familiar.

1. There are several instances in the Hebrew Bible where God makes a covenant with God's people (see Gen. 1:26-31; 3:16-19; 9:1-8; 12:1-4; 15:1-7, 17:1-8; Exod. 20:1-31; Deut. 30:1-10; 2 Sam. 7:4-16; Jer. 31:31-40).

- Whether a professional ecologist or a novice with a field guide in hand, when you have found what you are looking for, give it as much ecological attention as you can. You might want to use your field guide as an aid to help you journal, photograph, draw, or simply contemplate or explore your surroundings.
- As you are ready, let your senses and awareness enfold your object up to — and perhaps beyond — the point at which your awareness comes up against something "more" in nature than the material/ecological, something you can call mystery or wonder. Allow the mystery to unfold in you. Notice where your consciousness rests: with attentiveness, with mystery, or somewhere in balance.
- Exchange the word "God" with the word "nature" in the definitions of covenant above. What are possible covenants of wonder that you can form between yourself and nature? What covenants is nature making with you? What covenants can you make with nature? Are they conditional or unconditional?
- An example from Scripture that is a covenant not only with humanity but with the earth and all creatures of the earth is found in Genesis 9, where God sets an unconditional covenant with Noah and his descendents never again to destroy the earth with a flood. The sign of this covenant is also from nature, and is itself a wonder: a rainbow.
- How is your covenant with nature related to your "covenants" or your relationship with God?

PRACTICE 4.2

Wonder: Facing Nature, Facing Hope

INTENTION   Using the Christian theological or spiritual virtue of hope, the intention of this practice is to face nature with hope as a discipline of invitation, hospitality, participation, and gift.

PRACTICE   Jaco Hamman, a pastoral theologian, and a colleague and friend of mine, has formulated, from much more detailed work, a simple outline of Christian hope. Though not intended as such, his outline is comprehensive in a way that allows it to be applied to both humanity and creation. Hamman outlines Christian hope as follows:

1. Christian hope is rooted in the resurrection of Christ.

2. Hoping is a psychospiritual experience.
3. Hoping is not wishing.
4. Hoping is not willing.
5. Hoping anticipates some doubting, fearing, and even despairing.
6. Hoping requires surrendering to Someone bigger than you.
7. Hoping requires community.
8. Hoping always remembers a future.
9. Hoping has threats, stress points, and allies:

Threats	Stress Points	Allies
Despair	Fear	Trust
Apathy	Frustration	Patience
Shame	Failure	Modesty

- Go over the numbered elements of Christian hope, and in each case reflect on how these elements speak to your experience of hope. Pay particular attention to point 9, with its threats, stress points, and allies.
- Reflect a second time, using these same elements of Christian hope to explore how you experience hope with respect to nature. For example, using point 7, "Hoping requires community," you might reflect on the following:

  1. How do you experience nature as community? What are the attitudes, expectations, and/or prejudices about community through which we interpret nature?
  2. Pay close attention to the face of community that nature actually turns toward you. How does nature "present" community to you? How is this similar to and/or different from your expectations of community given above?
  3. Spend time with each of the threats, stress points, and allies of hope, in any order you wish. How do these affect your experience of community in creation?
  4. How does nature manifest hope, and how do you respond to this hope?

- Use each of the threats, stress points, and allies of hope as guides to how you experience hope in nature. How does (or doesn't) the face of nature inspire, solidify, encourage, or form trust and hope in you personally?
- Begin reflecting on how you might turn your hope into prayer and into earth-care.

Praising Like Queen Anne's Lace

[Full practice also in *Nature as Spiritual Practice*]

INTENTION The intention of this practice is to participate with nature in creation's constant doxology to the Creator. Saint Francis of Assisi observed and experienced nature as an intimate relationship. In Thoreau's words, only in such "intimate seeing," and not just "looking," was Saint Francis able to make the link between nature as family and nature as praise.

PRACTICE

- Creation teaches us to pray. Creation in prayer teaches us (1) to find a balance between being what we are created to be and doing what we are created to do; and, (2) within that balance, to abide in God's delight.
- Creation finds its own delight in leading us into such prayer. Look, find, and see how being present and open to nature allows nature to guide you in her ways of prayerful praise.
- Know whenever you face nature with attention and wonder that you are praising God, just as creation does the same.
- The psalmist writes: "Let the floods clap their hands; let the hills sing together for joy at the presence of the Lord" (Ps. 98:8). Watch, smell, feel something in nature: a river emptying into the ocean, the hills, the wine-purple floweret in the midst of white in Queen Anne's lace. Stay a moment to observe them clapping their hands, singing together with joy at the presence of the Lord. With practice, you will notice that nature is constantly praising God in this way.
- If, as Chief Sealth claims, nature is a web and you are a part of that web, simply in being yourself you give praise to God. How does what you do in nature — in that web — affect your relationship with God?

Belonging

INTENTION Knowing what the wolf knows, knowing what the mountain knows, sharing the wisdom and beauty of Queen Anne's lace, being named "My Delight Is in Her," and Chief Sealth's wisdom and his insight that "all things are connected" — all of these speak of one thing: belonging. The intention of this practice is to experience belonging in nature through the art of poetry.

PRACTICE

- Read the following poem by Mary Oliver twice, slowly (if in a group, let different people read in turn, two or three lines).

> You do not have to be good.
> You do not have to walk on your knees
> for a hundred miles through the desert, repenting.
> You only have to let the soft animal of your body
> love what it loves.
> Tell me about despair, yours, and I will tell you mine.
> Meanwhile the world goes on.
> Meanwhile the sun and the clear pebbles of the rain
> are moving across the landscapes,
> over the prairies and the deep trees,
> the mountains and the rivers.
> Meanwhile the wild geese, high in the clean blue air,
> are heading home again.
> Whoever you are, no matter how lonely,
> the world offers itself to your imagination,
> calls to you like the wild geese, harsh and exciting —
> over and over announcing your place
> in the family of things.[2]

- Having read the poem twice, take at most two minutes to write down a single word or phrase that is an image of what the poem means to you now. Do not censor yourself; respond to the first image that surfaces in you (if in a group, after the two minutes, invite anyone who would like to share the word or phrase with the larger group).
- Read the poem slowly and meditatively a third time.
- If in a group, break into groups of three. A good way to do this is to have all stand up, extend their elbows, find two people to touch each elbow thus creating a group of three standing close for intimate group discussion without violating personal space. Drop elbows and remain standing in circles of three.

2. Mary Oliver, "Wild Geese," in *Dream Work* (New York: Atlantic Monthly Press, 1986).

- Discuss among small groups — or journal if you are alone — your responses to the following two questions: (1) When do I feel the strongest sense of belonging to creation? (2) When do I feel the least sense of belonging to creation?
- If in a group, share some of your small-group responses.

Imprinted by Nature

INTENTION From an early age we are "imprinted," shaped, and formed by the land, by geography, climate, and the seasons. This practice is a simple experiment with the intention of helping us notice the early impact of place and ecology on our formation. We will notice how, in the process of this formation, nature imprints herself within us with a particular landscape or ecology that stays with us into adulthood and calls us with a longing and a sense of home.

PRACTICE In today's modern culture, most of us move from one place to another with some regularity. Between the time we are born and the time we die, most of us move at least once or twice; some people move from location to location around the world many times.

- Remember an early memory of place that makes a particular ecology feel most "natural" to you today, an environment and ecology where you would feel most at home. How old were you when you resided in this location? What kind of things did you do there that gave you pleasure? Think of geography, climate, plant and animal life, water, smells, and vistas — the sky and the contour of the earth. This is an ecology "imprinted" on your body, mind, and spirit.
- As you imagine yourself in this place, where would you most like to be and what would you most like to do?
- Now look around at the environment and ecology where you live now. If it is a new place (as for most of us it most likely is), how do you experience the new place in terms of your connection to nature? Compared to your memories and reflections of the first location, do you experience this newer geography and environment more as a loss, a gain, or an enhancement?
- A second part to this simple experiment is to ask these same questions

of a friend, listening carefully to her responses. Let that person recall and reminisce about her experiences and recollection of place from her youth.

- Next, just as you did for yourself, invite your friend to reflect on the environment and ecology where she lives now. Watch her closely. As she reflects on her new location, notice whether she appears more or less animated than when she reflected on her earlier location, more or less emotionally involved, more or less connected and at home. Ask her to make the comparison herself.
- Most people will show a marked emotional and spiritual preference for the imprint of an earlier environment and location.

The Book of Nature

CHAPTER FIVE

The Grammar of Nature

PRACTICE 5.1[1]

An Alphabet of Sound, The Language of Creation
[Full practice also in *Nature as Spiritual Practice*]

> The heavens are declaring the glory of God;
> and the firmament proclaims God's handiwork.
> Day to day pours forth speech,
> and night to night declares knowledge.
> There is no speech, nor are there words;
> their voice is not heard;
> yet their voice goes out through all the earth,
> and their words to the end of the world.
>
> Psalm 19:1-4

INTENTION   From Psalm 19 we learn that creation has its own language, a "speech" uttered in a "voice [that] goes out throughout all the earth." Creation's "voice is not heard," yet her "words" reach the ends of the cosmos. This practice is an exercise in listening as a condition of reading the book of nature. In it we will concentrate only on sound (just one way of "reading"). The intention of the practice is to be a simple primer for beginning to learn the language of the book of nature. A few responses from

---

1. This practice is based on an exercise, "The Poetics of Environmental Sound," developed by Pauline Oliveros in *The Book of Music and Nature*, ed. David Rothenberg and Marta Ulvaeus (Middletown, CT: Wesleyan University Press, 2001), 133-38.

others who practiced the exercise are included in order to help make this a collaborative listening project.

PRACTICE   Find a place in the natural world where you can listen uninterrupted for about thirty minutes.

- Listen to the environment for fifteen minutes or longer, but for a predetermined length of time. Use a timer, clock, or any adequate method to define this time length.
- Describe in detail the sounds you hear (heard) and how you feel (felt) about them (you may want to do this during the predetermined time or after). Write them in a notebook for yourself or for later sharing with a group.
- You are a part of the environment: include internal sounds as well as external sounds.
- Explore the limits of audibility (sounds that are highest/lowest, loudest/softest, simplest/most complex, nearest/most distant, longest/shortest).

SAMPLE RESPONSES
- "One thing I noticed right away was the absence of silence. There is always some kind of sound in the air."
- "I have just been in concert: the continuing concert of environmental sounds. I can hear it still."
- "Only a couple of minutes have passed and things are getting really involved already."
- "Five minutes have passed — only five minutes! Such a complex of varied sounds in such a short time. Well, onward — the sounds aren't waiting for me but are going on."
- "Sounds are very complex now. It is all but impossible to get them down; there seem to be a thousand things going on at once. Twelve minutes have passed."
- "I also noticed that my disposition was affected by the type of sounds I heard."

Scripture: An Out-of-Doors Book

INTENTION The intention of this practice is to read Scripture, with Wendell Berry's help, as an out-of-doors book: it is the story of creation, and it is best read open to the sky. When we read Scripture in this way, the miraculous is not the extraordinary but the common mode of existence; the common mode of existence can become extraordinary.

PRACTICE

- Wendell Berry has written this:

  I don't think it is enough appreciated how much an outdoor book the Bible is. It is a book open to the sky. It is best read and understood outdoors, and the farther outdoors the better. Or that has been my experience of it. Passages that within walls seem improbable or incredible, outdoors seem merely natural. That is because outdoors we are confronted everywhere with wonders; we see that the miraculous is not extraordinary, but the common mode of existence. Whoever really has considered the lilies of the field or the birds of the air, and pondered the improbability of their existence in this warm world within the cold empty stellar distances, will hardly balk at the changing of water into wine — which was, after all, a very small miracle. We forget the greater and still continuing miracle by which water (with soil and sunlight) is formed into grapes. . . . Holiness is everywhere in Creation; it is as common as raindrops and leaves and blades of grass.[2]

- Take this quote from Wendell Berry and your Bible and yourself to a special place in nature — outdoors.
- Still yourself and settle in. Expect miracles.
- Read the Berry quote again, then pick up your Bible and read, under the open sky, as Berry suggests.
- Read anything you would like. A few suggestions that are obviously about nature include: Genesis 1:1-25 or 1:26-31 or 2:10-15; Deuteronomy 8:2-10; Job 12:7-11; Job 38; Psalm 8:1-9; Psalm 104:1-28; Psalm 137; Proverbs 8:22-31; Isaiah 43:19-21; Matthew 17:1-2; Mark 1:35; Mark 6:46; Luke 19:39-40.

2. Wendell Berry, "Christianity and the Survival of Creation," *Cross Currents* 43, no. 2 (1993); online at www.crosscurrents.org/berry.htm (accessed March 2011).

- Other passages may call to you: Jesus' parables are peppered with nature images; any of the stories in the Gospels of Jesus feeding his followers (note the location, and note the fact that a major part of the sermon is centered on food, a gift of creation); Jesus healing the sick or raising Lazarus; Jesus meeting the woman at the well; Abraham about to sacrifice Isaac.
- Any passage is appropriate. But read it slowly and let the picture of the outdoors that it describes settle into you. Allow yourself self-guided meditation to imagine all you can about the natural world that the passage describes. Notice from Scripture or imagine weather, geography, dust, rocks, animals, plants, and the smells, sights, and sounds of nature and people.
- What, for you, is the relationship between nature and Scripture, and how does the one help you read and understand the other?
- Read a "miracle" story in Scripture, such as Jesus changing water to wine. Note the created elements of the story. Now meditate on the life cycle of a single plant or animal or even rock or river. How are these "ordinary" things "extraordinary" miracles no less than Jesus' changing of the water to wine?
- How does the "face" of nature change as you are reading Scripture outdoors? Notice what Scripture means to you, how you experience it, how it takes on a different energy or hue as you read it outdoors in the natural world.

PRACTICE 5.3

The Beatitudes and Reading Nature
[Full practice also in *Nature as Spiritual Practice*]

INTENTION   The intention of this practice is to use the Beatitudes as an example of reading nature through the "spectacles" of Scripture and virtue.

PRACTICE   The conclusion to *Nature as Spiritual Practice* is entitled "The Green Beatitudes." In that section we will look even more closely at the Beatitudes as model and guide for both contemplation of nature and virtue or earth-care in nature. As we work our way to the conclusion, begin to notice nature itself as an ideal point of balance between contemplation and virtue (or compassion). This point of balance between contemplation and virtue is a way of seeing God at the center of all things. The longer version of the Beatitudes, or the "Sermon on the Mount," is found in Matthew 5:3-11.

- Find a place in nature, settle in, notice your breath in order to become still, and read through Matthew's Beatitudes slowly several times. You may wish to use a practice that slows your reading to a meditative pace, such as *lectio divina.*
- As you are ready, read each Beatitude one at a time and pause after each, applying that saying to the natural world around you. It may help to imagine that Jesus' sermon is addressed to nature. This is not as odd as it may at first seem: Saint Francis of Assisi is famous for preaching to nature in just this way.
- Notice how each Beatitude can be applied to the natural world. Or, to put it another way, imagine the Beatitude as a special pair of glasses through which you observe nature. For example, the first Beatitude in Matthew 3:3 is: "Blessed are the poor in spirit, for theirs is the kingdom of heaven." Observe or walk through nature, watching for what you see or experience as "poor in spirit." This could be a dying or degraded part of nature; or "poor in spirit" can also mean "humble." What in nature is humble? One aspect of humility is simply being what one is created to be. How is a tree, for instance, being what it is created to be?
- How does what you see in nature as "poor in spirit" translate into a blessing?
- The Beatitudes are also virtues, ways of compassionate presence within the world. How do the Beatitudes translate into a compassionate way of being in the world? In the first Beatitude, for example, what would it mean for you to be "poor in spirit" in your interactions and connections with nature? How does behavior on your part that is "poor in spirit" bless nature?
- Go through each of the Beatitudes in the same way, pausing between each as long as you would like or are inspired to do so. You may wish to do each Beatitude on a different day or in a different location. Use a pace that is comfortable for you.

Ravens and Lilies: Care and Being Cared For

INTENTION The intention of this practice is to read the book of nature as a way of attending to and loving nature and to listen to the sermons of nature as a way of being loved and cared for by nature in return.

PRACTICE Read the following passage from Scripture slowly and meditatively three or four times. Note that in the second passage we are in fact invited to do just this: "consider," that is, meditate.

> "The wind blows where it chooses, and you hear the sound of it, but you do not know where it comes from or where it goes. So it is with everyone who is born of the spirit."
>
> John 3:8

> "Consider the ravens: they neither sow nor reap, they have neither storehouse nor barns, and yet God feeds them. . . . Consider the lilies, how they grow: they neither toil nor spin; yet I tell you, even Solomon in all his glory was not clothed like one of these."
>
> Luke 12:24, 27

Note the glory in the names themselves. They have not fallen into oblivion; rather, they burn with presence: "wind," "lilies," "ravens," "blows," "hear," "born," "barns."

- Spend time with the wind, and consider ravens and lilies. How do you read these things? Both passages above are short stories about God's sacred love and care for all creation. They are also stories about creation's habit of not worrying, but rather relying on nothing but God. Creation, confident of divine care, is free to give full attention and devotion to all that it is: the material as well as the sacred. What does nature teach you about meditation, consolation, trust, faith, and hope?
- Begin to read creation's book as a way of attending to nature with love. If the reading is difficult at first, don't be discouraged: Luke says, "God feeds them," and God will feed you.
- The wind, ravens, and lilies maintain a "clear remembrance of their Creator" and respond without hesitation to the love of God. For instance, the lily is a perfect response to the love of God calling it to be a lily. How

does creation's own attentive love of God help you to attend to and love creation (i.e., read its book)? How does creation help you attend to and love God (i.e., hear creation's sermon)?

- Here Christ is pointing to the natural world in order to "flesh out" his sermon or parable: the natural world itself becomes one of Christ's sermons. It is obvious that Christ has observed nature very closely, loving it and reading it as a book. It is also clear that Christ has heard the sermon of nature loving God in return. How can you best learn to hear the sermon of nature as Christ did?

- In Christ's parable in Luke, how is Christ urging us both to love nature and to be loved by nature?

- How does receiving nature on its own terms, as love for you, allow you to enter a reciprocating partnership with creation?

PRACTICE 5.5

Touched by a Tree
[Full practice also in *Nature as Spiritual Practice*]

INTENTION The intention of this practice is to "read" and "listen" to nature through the sense of touch. The sense of touch is unique. David Abram has written: "To touch the coarse skin of a tree is thus, at the same time, to experience one's own tactility, to feel oneself touched by the tree. And to see the world is also, at the same time, to experience oneself as visible, to feel oneself seen."[3]

PRACTICE Read again the quote about the Yup'ik hunter who listens and waits. We are not very good at listening to nature in this way. Find a place in creation to which you can give a fresh reading and where you can concentrate all your senses as you "touch" the sermon of creation in silence. Bring along something to eat.

- As Abram reminds us, to touch something with your hand provides a dual sensation: you will feel what you are touching and feel the feeling of being touched. Try it: rub your thumb and index finger together and you will feel each finger feeling and being felt. Feel nature. If, for example, you are touching a tree, notice that as you touch and feel the bark,

---

3. David Abram, *The Spell of the Sensuous: Perception and Language in a More-than-Human World* (New York: Pantheon Books, 1996), 68.

at the same time you sense yourself feeling the touch of the bark. Though we seldom notice, this is the case with everything we touch or feel.

- Try noticing touch and being touched at the same time. Do you move back and forth between being aware of touch and being touched, or do you sense both simultaneously?
- Taste is very much a tactile sense: touch is essential to taste. Take a bite of fruit or whatever you brought with you. As you taste an apple, for instance, notice how you taste the apple while at the same time you feel the apple in your mouth. Can you separate this tactile sense from the taste itself?
- Sight, if we grant that the "other" is also a subject and loved by God (Heb. 1:3), also sees and is seen. Look closely at something in nature. How is nature seeing *you* in return?
- Find a fragrance in nature and try shutting off your other senses and concentrating on the fragrance. As you inhale the fragrance, how do you experience yourself taking in the odor? Is it a dual sense as is touch?
- Finally, listening and hearing also lend themselves to Lopez's plea for renewed attention to the wisdom of the earth. Listen to yourself hearing nature.
- Spend time practicing different ways to experience these dual capacities of all your senses in nature.

PRACTICE 5.6

Nature's Parts of Speech

INTENTION The intention of this practice is to begin to (re)learn the language of creation at a grammatical level by noticing how nature can be seen and interpreted — metaphorically and literally — in terms of parts of speech, such as verbs, nouns, adverbs, and adjectives. This is a practice of listening, noticing, and granting nature its language.

Stories with animals are older than history and better than philosophy. History tries to describe the world as if it began with writing and only humans mattered; philosophy attempts to abstract truth as if it were defined only by discursive thought and experience of the natural world were unimportant. Speech . . . permits us to recapitulate experience to one another in ways that make sense of a world where the others communicate — tell their stories — differently.

Paul Shepard[4]

PRACTICE   Read the Paul Shepard quote above once again and read over once more what Ann Whiston Spirn has to say about language and landscape in the chapter. This practice is an interactive meditation.

- Watch and listen for "verbs" in nature: watching for movement in a river or a path, for example, is the easiest way to enter into nature as "verb." Other possibilities are the verb of the movement of wind through trees or the settling of a moth on a flower. Use your creative imagination.
- What can you perceive as nouns? The same water, path, leaves, wind, moth might be agents and objects. Again, "read" nature slowly and meditatively, using your senses and imagination to see these same objects in this different — grammatical — sense.
- Shift to adjectives and adverbs. These may include wet, green, wide, or blessed as adjectives or slowly, broadly, sadly, or brightly as adverbs.
- In each of these, take your time. You are (re)learning a language, but nature is a good teacher.
- Now practice putting together short phrases. Watch the setting sun as a verb, to which you attach an adverb from nature that reflects your mood. For instance, you may notice shadows as "sadly" attached to the verb of the setting sun: "It is the time of the sadly setting sun."
- Perhaps you can now put a sentence together, perhaps even forgetting the grammar as we do when we are proficient at reading. "The sadly setting sun blues this river of cloud."
- Shepard does not mention "silence" or "listening" as story, or as a means of "recapitulating experience," but silence does speak. What does silence from animals or plants or earth "speak" to you?

4. Paul Shepard, *The Others: How Animals Made Us Human* (Washington, DC: Island Press, 1996), 90.

CHAPTER SIX

The Sacred Idiom of Nature

The Sacred Idiom of Psalm 104

INTENTION The natural world is a sacred idiom that is formative of Christian identity. The intention of this practice is to read nature through Psalm 104, and then Psalm 104 through nature, noting what each reading helps us to remember about ourselves and about God.

PRACTICE Take a walk in nature or find a place where you can return over the next few days or weeks. Go there and follow nature's guidance. Again, you may wish to journal, photograph, draw, consult a field guide, or simply wander.

- After wandering in nature, read Psalm 104 meditatively several times, even over several days. You can do this initially indoors, then move outdoors.
- When you have absorbed the psalm, return to that place in nature where you wandered at the beginning of this practice.
- Notice the effect that reading Psalm 104 has had on how you experience the world? How is the "language" of nature different from your first experience?
- Another way to notice the effect of Psalm 104 on your experience in nature is to reflect on what you might have heard and seen in nature had you stepped into creation after having done something else, such as

reading the paper, eating, watching television, interacting personally or on the Internet, studying, or even praying.

- On another occasion, enter the natural world as you normally would: hiking, camping, canoeing, watching. At the end of your time in nature, read Psalm 104. In this case, what takes place in the "opposite" direction? That is, what is the effect on your experience of nature during or after you read Psalm 104?
- Do you find more it more meaningful for you to read nature through the psalm or the psalm through nature?
- The end of verse 13 of Psalm 104 reads: ". . . the earth is satisfied with the fruits of God's works." Reflect on how you experience the earth satisfied and happy with God's works. How has humanity made it difficult or impossible for the earth to be satisfied with the fruits of God's works, or to be a referent for God's sacred idiom?

PRACTICE 6.2

The Oblivion of Names

INTENTION The intention of this practice is both to cherish names as they give reality to the things of creation and, on the other hand, to experience how the forgetting of names of things of creation is equivalent to forgetting the things themselves, as well as their Creator.

PRACTICE Read this short quote taken from the larger quote from Cormac McCarthy: "The names of things slowly following those things into oblivion." Read the quote slowly several times over. The practice can be done indoors or out, but the most effective use of the practice is in the natural world.

- "The names of things slowly following those things into oblivion." Give yourself space and time to meditate on and remember as many names of things in creation as you can. In nature, notice all that is around you and name it: if you do not know the name of the species, simply name what you see, for instance, "tree" or "bird."
- Now, do the same (you may notice more names); but this time, as each name comes to you, imagine the name falling slowly into oblivion, that is, imagine the forgetting of that name and the lack of importance of names in a story like McCarthy's. Imagine the effect of the oblivion of

names on the thing itself. What does it mean for a thing in nature to be, but without a name?

- As the names fall into oblivion, next imagine the created thing itself falling into oblivion. In other words, imagine something from creation becoming "extinct" as its name falls into oblivion. Does some shadow of the name linger after the "extinction"? Let even that shadow fall into oblivion.

- How do you experience God in this nameless world? The true name of God is difficult to render. What if God had no name?

- Over the millennia many species have become extinct, and today species are becoming extinct at an alarming rate. They are falling into oblivion, and as they do, their names will eventually fall into oblivion with them. A recent book gives a statistic indicating that a species of plant or animal becomes extinct every eight hours. That is three species per day. Recall a few species that have recently become extinct or are close to extinction. What do you feel about their absence and loss? What added sorrow or loss do humans experience as their names sink into oblivion?

- Everything around you in creation has a name. If you don't know the name, you do know that it has a name, and that you can find out what it is. Find something in nature whose name you know. How does the name limit your experience of this object? How does it enhance it? Can you experience this thing without being conscious of its name?

PRACTICE 6.3

Listening with Fresh Ears[1]
[Full practice also in *Nature as Spiritual Practice*]

INTENTION   The intention of this practice is to bring fresh ears to the task of listening to the silence, the names, and the sonic language of nature.

PRACTICE   This practice can be done indoors or outdoors. The questions are helpful for learning, over time, to "hear" nature in every sense. Go over the following questions and allow them to open doors into new ways of perceiving (or reading) creation.

---

1. This practice is adapted from Pauline Oliveros, "Sonic Images," in *The Book of Music and Nature: Anthology of Sounds, Words, Thoughts,* ed. David Rothenberg and Marta Ulvaeus, copyright © Wesleyan University Press, 1995, 130-33. Used by permission of Wesleyan University Press.

- Can you find the quiet place in your mind where there are no thoughts, no words, and no images?
- Can you remain in this quiet mind place by listening to all the sounds you can possibly hear, including the most distant sounds beyond the space you now occupy?
- Do you ever notice how your ears adjust inside when you move from one size space to another? Or from indoors to outdoors, or vice versa?
- What is your favorite sound? Can you reproduce it in your mind? Would you communicate to someone else what your favorite sound is?
- Have you heard a sound lately that you could not identify? What were the circumstances? How did you feel?
- What do you sound like when you walk?
- Imagine the sound of a bird call. What kind of bird is it? When did you last hear it? What does it sound like? Can you imitate it?
- What is the most silent period you have ever experienced? Was it only a moment, or was it very long? What was its effect on you?
- What is the most complex sound you have ever experienced? What were the circumstances and how did you feel?

PRACTICE 6.4

The Blind See

INTENTION The intention of this two-part practice is to experience "blindness" in order to "see" creation in new, often surprising ways that can help us become postmodern indigenous Christians.

PRACTICE Those who are blind learn to hear in different ways. Listen to John Hull, who is blind, speak of what he "sees" of the landscape as he listens to falling rain: "Rain has a way of bringing out the contours of everything. . . . Here and there is a light cascade as it drips from step to step. . . . I can even make out the contours of the lawn, which rises to the right in a little hill. The sound of the rain is different and shapes out the curvature for me. . . . Everywhere are little breaks in the patterns, obstructions, projections, where some slight interruption or difference of texture or of echo gives an additional detail or dimension to the scene."[2] The composer Fran-

2. John M. Hull, *Touching the Rock: An Experience of Blindness* (New York: Vintage, 1992), 29-30.

cisco López writes: "In most cases — especially forests — what we tend to refer to as the sound of rain or wind might more aptly be called the sound of plant leaves and branches. . . . The birdsong we hear in the forest is as much a consequence of the trees of the forest as it is of the bird."[3]

There are two practices that, even in being "blind" for a short time, help us see creation in new ways.

1. Trust and Blindness

- This first practice combines your trust of another person and "blindness" to help you feel and hear nature more intensely.
- This simple practice is done either with a group or one other person. If with a group, divide into pairs. Do the practice in any area of creation that is open to explore with the senses.
- One partner closes his eyes or is blindfolded. The other partner, the guide, holds the arm or hand of the "blind" partner and leads him through creation, gently guiding steps and direction so that the "blind" partner feels safe in his environment.
- The guide directs the "blind" partner in an exploration of touch and hearing. As guide, she leads the "blind" partner to various objects and allows him to explore these objects with touch: leaves, grass, rocks, tree trunks, and flowers. She allows the "blind" partner to explore as long as he chooses to, then moves on to another object.
- The guide and the "blind" partner can also be listening. Remain quiet as needed, but allow the "blind" partner to share characteristics of the sound as he wishes: where it comes from, what is making it, how you can "see" the landscape as John Hull describes it.
- Explore in this way for an allotted amount of time — thirty minutes is good — then switch roles and repeat the process for the same amount of time.
- At the end of the practice, partners discuss together what they experienced in touch and sound and what the earth looks like now — that is, after the practice.

2. Blind, Sensing Jesus

- In her autobiography, Teresa of Avila complains that "discursive meditation" (a proscribed and very rational, linear form of meditation popular at the time) does her no good. She just doesn't get it. As an alternative,

---

3. Francisco López, "Blind Listening," in Rothenberg and Ulvaeus, *Book of Music and Nature*, 162.

Teresa proposes a more imaginative, creative form of prayer that she finds effective and that brings her solace. Her alternative practice is that she closes her eyes and sits in her room just as it is, while she imagines that she is blind. Keeping her eyes closed, she imagines Jesus entering the room and uses her other senses to "feel" his presence. In the eyes of her heart she sees him approach, touch her, and she talks with him. She simply lets this meditative prayer go where it will while she continues to remain "blind," but together with Jesus. Finally, she imaginatively senses Jesus blessing her and taking his leave. This prayer seems always to bring a freshness to her image of Jesus and her sense of his continual presence.

- Find a place in the natural world where things are moving or there are sounds you may not be able to identify but can hear.
- Close your eyes and imagine that you are blind.
- Reflect on how you experience nature around you and how sound approaches. Can you sense shapes, branches, humidity, and movement simply through sound, as John Hull does?
- Now, just as Teresa of Avila does in her room, imagine Jesus walking up beside you in nature while you are still blind. Sense and feel his presence. Let him touch you. Talk with him about what you notice in nature while you are "blind." Or you may simply want to sit in silence with him, sharing his presence with creation.
- Imagine Jesus taking his leave, and as he does so, offering his blessing.

PRACTICE 6.5

Nature and Scripture Converse
[Full practice also in *Nature as Spiritual Practice*]

INTENTION   The intention of this practice is to sit in the midst of the conversation between nature and Scripture, and to begin to experience this conversation as Christ did.

PRACTICE   You will need a Bible and an object of nature that has special meaning for you (shell, rock, feather, bird's nest, tree, etc.). It is best to do this practice with a companion.

- Read the following from Saint Augustine aloud: "Some people, in order to discover God, read books. But the whole Trinity is revealed to us in creation. There is a great book: the very appearance of created things.

Look above you! Look below you! Note it! Read it! God, whom you want to discover, never wrote that book with ink. Instead God set before your eyes the things that He had made. Can you ask for a louder voice than that? Why, heaven and earth shout to you: 'God made me!'"[4]

- Place your object from nature on the floor if you're inside, or on the ground if you're outside; or if it's large, such as a tree, sit some distance from it.

- If you are alone, journal; if you are with a companion, write or speak together about the object from nature. Say anything that comes to mind about what it is speaking to you of itself, of you, of your companion, and of God.

- Journal or talk with your companion also about what you each think is the still point, the center of your being as you sit, and what resides there.

- After some time, read Psalm 104, Psalm 148, a portion of the Song of Songs, or any other selection from Scripture that speaks to you in a particularly intense way about nature.

- When the reading is done, place the Bible, open to the passage you have read, on the floor or ground some distance from your object. Say aloud — or make conscious in some personal way — the fact that the object from nature and Scripture are in conversation. You may wish to pray that you become aware of, or part of, this conversation as it takes place.

- Sit quietly, imagining and listening to the conversation between this object from creation and the Scripture you have just read, and which is now present in the silence. From time to time you may wish to reread either Scripture or your object in order to keep current in the conversation.

- As you are ready, become aware of the space between the object from nature and the Bible, the space that is a circle of conversation, containing power and blessing and the fire of God. Recognize this space as Christ.

- Alone or with your companion, move into the space between the object and the Bible; hold hands together, pray whatever comes to your heart; and be present to the Spirit in Christ and in you as the sacred matters, here and now, in this conversation between Scripture and nature.

4. Augustine, from quotations compiled by Fred Krueger, "Opening the Book of Nature.Com": http://www.bookofnature.org/library/ngb.html (accessed April 2009).

Creation Contemplation

CHAPTER SEVEN

Nature as Liturgy and Prayer

PRACTICE 7.1

Creation Contemplation

INTENTION Prayer is a lifetime practice; creation contemplation is a way of life. The intention of this practice is to experience the five types of creation prayer or contemplation listed below.

PRACTICE This practice is a contemplative prayer of attentive wonder. Most fundamentally, creation contemplation is a prayer of connection between creation, humanity, and God. Reread the short section in the preface to *Nature as Spiritual Practice* entitled "Reawakening Attention, Wonder, and Moral Response." Look again at the five modes of creation contemplation listed in chapter 7:

1. Creation's contemplation of or prayer to God
2. Humanity's contemplation of or prayer to God through creation
3. God's own loving contemplation of creation
4. Creation as a manifestation of God's contemplation
5. Reciprocal prayer between creation and humanity as prayer to God

PREPARATION This practice intends to "triangulate" (in a good sense) creation, God, and humanity in the context of the various forms of contemplative prayer, and it requires more preparation than most. You will need your Bible throughout. Allow creation to guide you in this practice; pray along with creation in the form in which you are most comfortable.

Since this is a lifelong practice, you may want to begin by reading the Song of Songs. This book will stir and awaken your senses and heart to the natural world as a sensual place of intimacy, affection, and connection.

Begin by writing down all you can think of or can notice about how creation, humanity, and God are in prayer in these five modes. Then proceed slowly through the material below for all five of the modes slowly — at your own pace, over time.

1. *Creation's contemplation of God.* The constant prayer of creation to God is something we recognize initially in "pieces," but over time we begin to recognize as a constant prayer. An excellent way to enter into this prayer is by meditating on Psalm 19 or Psalm 148. Psalms 72, 95–100, 104 are just a few illustrations of the love of creation for her Creator in melodies of praise. Notice, for example, that in Psalm 96, God's creation is such that "all earth" praises God. In Psalm 19, the heavens proclaim God's glory while the sun (a symbol of God) comes out like a bridegroom to the earth as bride. The Psalter is not the only book in Scripture to praise God's glory in and through creation. Read, for instance, Isaiah 42 and Sirach 42 and 43. Of course, creation contemplation is not all praise. In Romans 1, creation "groans." Allow yourself to join creation as she guides you into all forms of prayer: praise, thanksgiving, intercession, lament, attention, and giving glory to God simply by being what we are (a stone being a stone, a tree being a tree, you simply being you).

2. *Humanity's contemplation of God through creation.* This is the form of creation prayer modeled by Saint Francis of Assisi in his "Canticle of Creatures." The Canticle is readily available in print or on the Internet. The first thing most people notice about the Canticle is that humanity is not separate from creation but is, in fact, a part of the family of creation: we are sisters, brothers, daughters, and sons of creation. For Saint Francis, humanity — through *all* of creation — receives the gift and blessing of prayer to God. Read Francis's Canticle and, after a time, find how you are guided and drawn to praying to God through creation. In Scripture, the book of Jonah — from leviathans to storms to shade-giving vines — is an extended contemplative prayer of the presence of God through creation (though, as often as not, Jonah would prefer that God not be present, at least not for a while!). Nearly all of Jesus' parables involve images of nature: they are, in effect, perfect

prayers to God through the medium of creation, prayers that we are invited to imitate.

3. *God's loving contemplation of creation.* God's is a constant, contemplative prayer of longing and love that brings into being, sustains, and preserves creation. God's first prayer concerning creation was simply this: "It is good" (Gen. 1). Jumping to the book of Acts, creation is not only sustained, but it also serves as a witness and testimony of divine prayer: "[Y]et God has not left himself without a witness in doing good — giving you rains from heaven and fruitful seasons, and filling you with food and your hearts with joy" (Acts 14:17). Since the Enlightenment, we have been trained to perceive creation as an object with properties that can be measured, calibrated, and put to good use. There is nothing wrong with this, except that in so measuring it, we have desensitized ourselves to creation as an ongoing prayer of God. We have removed ourselves from what David Abram calls "the spell of the sensuous." Opening our eyes to divine love as an equally "real" property of, say, a stone, is to encounter God at prayer within creation. Psalm 104 also illuminates God the Creator as the prayerful, loving provider, protector, and sustainer of creation. Another way of perceiving God in contemplation of nature is found in Colossians 1, where the creative love of God takes shape as ongoing prayer of reconciliation and redemption. In Colossians, Christ is the "image of the firstborn of creation": "He himself is before all things, and in him all things hold together," while "through Christ God was pleased to reconcile to himself all things, whether on earth or in heaven" (Col. 1:15, 17, 20). The book of Hebrews also points toward this divine prayer: "Through Christ all things are sustained" (Heb. 1:3). Sabbath, too, is the response of a contemplative Creator, not only to the Creator's need for rest, but for all of creation's needs as well (Exod. 23:12), while every seventh year, in like manner, the land is also prayed into Sabbath rest (Exod. 23:10-11; Lev. 25:2).

Commandments and precepts are not intended to suppress or confine humanity; they are intended as guides to wisdom and blessings, the meditation of which provide humanity with a vehicle of return to God. In Scripture, though they are often conditional, the "condition" of successful observance of divine laws is reflected in creation's abundance: "If you follow my statutes and keep my commandments and observe them faithfully, I will give you your rains in their season, and the land shall yield its produce, and the trees of the field shall yield their fruit" (Lev. 26:3-4). "The compassion of the Lord is for every living thing" (Sirach 18:13a). Because of God's compassionate prayer for all creation, all creation is streaked in glory: "I will now call to mind the works of the Lord, and will declare what I have seen. By the word of the Lord his works are made; and all his creatures do his will. The sun looks down on everything with its light, and the work of the Lord is full of his glory" (Sirach 42:15-16; see also Sirach 43; Ps. 33).

4. *Creation as a manifestation of God's contemplation.* Begin to notice and walk and dwell in creation as the manifestation of God's own divine contemplation, that is, that the earth is the material/ecological evidence of God's own sacred contemplations. This will change your perception of the earth: the grasses are physical manifestations of divine contemplation; mountains are the contemplation of God; our neighbors glow as realities of God's loving contemplation. This does not mean that creation is simply the "mind of God." That is too simplistic and does not do justice to either creation or God. Lie on your back on the earth: the sky and clouds, light, soil, trees, breath, grass, that earthy smell, bird songs — all these are in and of themselves divine prayer. If this is difficult at first, let God and creation guide you. "God is love, and those who abide in love abide in God, and God abides in them" (1 John 4:16).

5. *Reciprocating contemplative prayer between creation and humanity.* Contemplation — running both ways, between humanity and creation — is explicit in Scripture. Contemplation in this sense is mutual, cumulative, and reciprocal. Though often neglected today, creation is in a reciprocal, symmetrical relationship of prayer with humans. Some may experience this relationship as asymmetrical (most often asymmetry is displayed in disproportionate love flowing through creation to humanity). But the importance of this reciprocating prayer is that, together, nature and humanity (not just humanity) are a part of God's work of reconciliation. Throughout Scripture we find God wholly in the business of reconciliation: through Christ, God reconciles all things to Godself; God will be all in all; all God created is good; we are created through the Word of God; creation itself awaits with eager longing for the redemption and reconciliation of all children of creation to God. Another way this prayer is seen is in the way humanity and creation are related in Genesis 2:15. This passage, if translated literally, goes something like this: "The Lord God took the man and caused him to rest in the garden of Eden, to serve *(abad)* it and to keep

(shamar) it." "Serve" is often translated here as "work" or "till." And the word for "keep" indicates a loving, caring, sustaining kind of keeping. Creation "keeps," loves, cares for, and sustains in return — in those sensuous spaces between caring and keeping. Still another illustration is that of the role of Wisdom in Proverbs. In Proverbs 8:22-30, Wisdom rejoices equally and in the same way in the creation of the universe and in the creation of humanity. The marks of Wisdom in nature become entry points of contemplative prayer.

One way to help enter into creation contemplation is to pray Paul's attributes of love as he offers them in 1 Corinthians 13. If we, over time, participate in the five modes of creation prayer, if we are enveloped in any of the attributes from Paul's list, we will begin to open our selves, creation, and God to prayer as it was in the beginning, is now, and will be forever. Paul says that love —

- Is patient
- Is kind
- Is not envious or boastful or arrogant or rude
- Does not insist on its own way
- Is not irritable or resentful
- Does not rejoice in wrongdoing
- Rejoices in truth
- Bears all things
- Believes all things
- Hopes all things
- Endures all things
- Never ends

In Psalm 97:4, "the earth sees." In Genesis, all creation is proclaimed by God to be "good." In the Gospel of John, "God so loved the world." In seeing goodness and in love of creation, humanity and God remain in prayer.

PRACTICE 7.2

The Liturgy of Creation

INTENTION This section suggests that the cycles, movements, and elements of nature are themselves ritual and liturgy. As with participation in any ritual or liturgy, participation with the liturgy of creation forms and transforms identity and consciousness. Over the centuries, the church's liturgical calendar has been marked off in "seasons." The intention of this practice is (1) to notice the many cycles of nature and to experience the formational qualities of the liturgy of creation; and (2) to witness and participate in the larger worship or liturgical practices of the church transposed to nature.

PRACTICE   First, make a point of finding out the liturgical seasons that your church celebrates (or does not celebrate!) and the current season of the liturgy. There is a reason we refer to these as liturgical "seasons": initially, they were very consciously associated with a particular season in nature. Liturgical seasons can be slow or drawn out, so this practice is an opportunity to participate in liturgical seasons of creation that are very short in duration and those that are much longer. Other common aspects of liturgy are the building blocks of any church's worship.

1. Formational Cycles of Nature and Their Relation to the Church Calendar
- Having explored the liturgical seasons of your own church and how they are celebrated, remember back on what various liturgical seasons of the church have meant to you. Church liturgical seasons vary widely, but a few that are nearly universally celebrated include Advent, Lent, Easter, the Ascension, and Ordinary Time. If you have participated in a church that recognizes these liturgical seasons, how has your experience of them shaped and formed your sense of self, your relationship to the church, your identification with other participants, and your sense of divine presence?
- Journal these experiences or share them in a trusted group.
- After you have clarified the meaning and experience of the church's liturgical year, begin to notice some of the many liturgical rituals of nature. At their most basic, these will include movement, transformation, and changes or cycles in nature. You can expect to give your own meaning to creation liturgy, so you should be open to the process and should bring your own imagination and creativity to the rituals of nature.
- The cycles you will begin to notice may be very swift, such as the movement of river water across stone or a wolf slipping away in the periphery of your vision. Or they may be moderate, like the movement of clouds across the sky or a leaf falling from a tree. Or they may be violent, like earthquakes or weather systems. They may be regular, pre-

dictable, and reassuring, such as the rising of the sun or the phases of the moon; or they may be relatively long, such as the seasons of the year or the year itself; or they may be imperceptible and very, very long, but nonetheless taking place, such as the slow erosion of a mountain or retreat of a glacier; or they may be unimaginably long, such as the birth, life, and death of a star.

- How does your particular setting in nature affect how you experience her cycles and liturgies? How does light or shadow shift and change? What is happening because of the particular season and place you are in? Life and death themselves are liturgical cycles, celebrated in the church as the occasions of the Nativity and Good Friday. How are the rituals of degeneration and renewal in nature happening around you?

- Once you begin to notice the rituals of creation, imagine how you or a small group can begin to transform these natural rituals into liturgies. One way to get started is to use the church's liturgical seasons and apply them to nature. What cycles in nature are perpetually renewing, giving birth, or returning in a special way — which is a central message of Advent? What dies in order that something else may live, which represents central messages of Lent, Good Friday, and Easter? The longest church liturgical season is Ordinary Time. What in nature is "ordinary time"? Remember that, as liturgy, "ordinary time" is made "extraordinary" in its ordinariness.

- Another way of joining or witnessing the liturgy of creation is to return to the same place over time in order to notice slower, seasonal changes. This can be enhanced by photographing a particular spot during different times of the year.

- You may choose to witness creation's ritual as formal and carefully choreographed, like the slow rotation of stars through the sky; or it may seem random and playful, like waves on an ocean shore. In either case, give yourself permission to experience each as a form of liturgical worship. Depending on your tradition, this may involve formal precision or spontaneous response.

2. Worship and Creation Liturgy

- The effective differences between the liturgical calendar and liturgical worship are more a matter of substance and duration than of kind or difference in formational quality. For churches that follow the rhythm of the liturgical calendar, that calendar is put to practice in liturgical worship; for churches that do not follow the liturgical year, worship is built up of liturgical elements. These liturgical rituals include anything you might see on a given Sunday in your order of worship: call to worship, apostolic greeting, *Gloria Patri,* public confession, assurance of pardon, responsive reading, Scripture reading, sermon or meditation, Lord's Supper/Mass, doxology, benediction, and, of course, hymns and singing. Dance is being revived as a liturgical practice, while marriage, ordination, funerals, and other ceremonies have their liturgical elements.

- All of these elements of worship find their counterparts in creation. Explore, wander, journal, photograph, or in other ways pay attention to creation as you experiment with these different orders of worship and how nature exhibits her own related liturgical qualities.

- Examples might include nature calling to you in a particular way into worship: for example, any water is a natural liturgical reminder of baptism. Ask yourself how nature delivers her benediction to you.

- Find a way to participate in the nature liturgy you find. You can also create your own liturgical worship elements within nature as you find them. A former student of mine offers the following way of worship that she remembers as a child. The worship incorporates creation into its informal liturgy: "Out-of-doors, the chairs would be arranged in a circular style with the preacher and choir being a part of the service. We would use things in nature as our instruments. We would have the sounds of rocks, which were placed in a box, or sea shells mixed with sand and sticks in a box. The sound of the water was an active part of the worship service. The wind or lack of wind was an immediate reminder of the presence of God in nature, especially as one would lie down on the sand after dancing in the Holy Spirit. I can remember the feel of the sand as one kicked off shoes and danced around calling on the name of Jesus, and how the smell of the water would give me an opportunity to experience God outside of my body. The cries of mercy, sounds of endless prayers, and shouts of joy were carried in the wind. As a youth, I wondered where those sounds finally found a home. And even the seagulls joined the choir to sing praises to our Lord."

- You may wish to develop a worship service or liturgy appropriate to a particular place in nature adapted for a particular purpose. For instance, table fellowship in the form of the Eucharist or Lord's Supper, or of a simple meal, is appropriate and can center the liturgy. Find ways to share the elements not only with the human participants but also with creation: animals, plants, birds, earth, and sky — as each one also participates in this liturgy.

Holy Now

[Full practice also in *Nature as Spiritual Practice*]

INTENTION

The intention of this practice is to awaken our consciousness to the miracles that surround us everywhere in nature.

PRACTICE   Online, go to URL http://www.petermayer.net/music/?id=4, where you will find the complete lyrics to Peter Mayer's song "Holy Now," from his album *Million Dollar Mind*. The song is also available for downloading from your favorite music website.

- Read the complete lyrics or, better, download Mayer's song; listen and enjoy. After reading or listening to the song several times, take a walk in the natural world with attentive wonder and focus on the ordinary, yet noting the extraordinary.
- Remember that you are connecting to the prayer of nature. This prayer becomes your own prayer of wonder as you begin to see creation as God's miraculous, continuous prayer.
- Ask yourself whether a tree is a miracle. Are its leaves prayer? As a way of seeing that everything is a miracle, practice trying to find what in nature is not miracle or prayer. If you are truly open to nature prayer and your own prayer of the earth, you will find it difficult to find something in creation that is not prayer — even death. The possible exception to this is areas of creation degraded by humanity.
- After a time, you will see that walking on the earth as prayer shapes attention, wonder, hope, and faith in a way that makes a stone no less miraculous than the birth of a fawn.

No Sign but Everything That Is

[Full practice also in *Nature as Spiritual Practice*]

> The Incarnate Word is with us,
> is still speaking — is present
> always, yet leaves no sign
> but everything that is.

Wendell Berry, "Sabbaths, 1999," IX[1]

INTENTION   In this practice we "go back to school," and the teacher will be creation herself. Intentions include learning to meditate on and listen to the conversation of creation and to develop and exercise your own way of entering contemplative prayer with the natural world.

PRACTICE

- Begin this practice by praying that the divine will guide you as you begin to learn the language of creation. As you begin, remember to approach nature in ways that are most life-giving to you: sitting, walking, camping, canoeing, sitting in a city park, getting lost in the desert, journaling, photographing, or just wandering.
- Reflect on Erasmus's translation of John 1:1: "In the beginning was the conversation." How does the idea of creation coming into being through "conversation" rather than "word" affect your relationship to nature?
- Begin to imagine that all you perceive around you was born from holy conversation and is, in fact, a continuous conversation between creation and God. How does this affect your image of God? What does it mean for how you can participate in this conversation as prayer?
- Notice that Berry uses the image of the "Incarnate Word" in his poem. But Berry also implies that this incarnation, this enfleshment, is less a single word than an ongoing conversation. More than that, the "Incarnate Conversation" is ever present: Berry says that this conversation leaves no sign — except everything that exists. Consider, journal, photograph, paddle, or camp your way into how this might be a poetic way of speaking of the miraculous in the everyday for you.

---

1. Wendell Berry, in *Given Poems* (Emeryville, CA: Shoemaker and Hoard, 2005), 78.

- If the "Incarnate Conversation" speaks in signs through everything that is in creation, how does this affect your relationship with nature? Your contemplative prayer in and with nature? Your connection with God?

PRACTICE 7.5

Contemplative Prayer as Stalking Mystery

INTENTION The intention of this practice is to enter into creation contemplation, paying very careful attention by "stalking" in nature — perhaps a deer, perhaps a wildflower — and then to notice the shift from stalking the object to stalking mystery, and the shift from stalking into an ephemeral and enduring prayer of creation.

PRACTICE Bill Plotkin is a gifted teacher and writer in the art of paying attention to creation itself and the mystery that creation both conceals and reveals. Below are a few methods for "stalking" creation that Plotkin teaches. Read the following and begin stalking! Give yourself the time and opportunity to stalk mystery in nature.

- Skillful nature observation requires your willingness to sit motionless for long periods and focus on what is in front and around and inside of you, bringing your attention always back to the present moment. Look with care. Look into things, not just at them. Listen to the texture of sound as well as its origin and volume. Track scent as well as color and shifting shade. Become acquainted with the feel of surfaces as well as the touch of wind and stillness, the dance of warmth and chill.
- Be truly curious. Observe with innocence and delight. In addition to the behavior of animals and insects and the movement of vegetation, there is a lively life of the air and sky, the flow of water and light. Some things you will learn by sitting still (one method of stalking); some by tracking slowly (another method of stalking); some by returning to the same spot time and again over different seasons and many years, getting to know not just the species there but also the individual animals and plants.
- In offering your attention generously, you discover astonishing things: secret gardens; insect worlds; the shape, feel, and traveling modes of seeds; the way the wind behaves in different spaces; the way moving sunlight plays tricks on the mind; the sound of hoof and paw on rock

and on dry leaves. You discover your own emotions, losses, unexpected identities, and destinies.

- In spending an hour or more tracking an animal or flower, you gradually shift your consciousness. While you are focused on the outer, elusive presence, changes happen on the inside: you quiet down; life becomes simpler; you come to belong more fully to the place you wander, following a track or scent or sound. Eventually, you notice "being on the track" is its own reward, just as life is more about the journey than the destination.

- You may begin by stalking deer, but notice how you are captivated by surprises of any kind, including shifts in your own consciousness and new subjects as you stalk. "You might continue with the deer track because that is the path you chose at the start . . . [yet] you notice that you are incrementally becoming someone who stalks a mystery. Something in you is changing. . . . What is the secret place inside from which you sense the mystery, the place from which you long for the trail as much as the treasure?"[2]

- We all pray differently. As you stalk in nature, how does this become the kind of prayer that is unique to your personality, desires, and gifts?

PRACTICE 7.6

The Sacrament of Silence

INTENTION   The intention of this practice is to experience silence in creation as sacramental.

PRACTICE   The website "Web of Creation" offers the following reflection on the sacramental quality of nature. The website, after reflecting on the elements from nature connected with baptism and the Lord's Supper — water, wheat, grape, each incarnate in their own ways — continues:

> *The Sacramental Presence of God Everywhere.* Finally, it is important to observe that the elements of the sacraments are "common" elements of life — elements of food upon which we depend for life — assuring us that if God can be present in and through such common elements as bread and wine, then surely God is present to us every-

2. Bill Plotkin, *Soulcraft: Crossing into the Mysteries of Nature and Psyche* (Novato, CA: New World Library, 2003), 178-79.

where in life. What difference does it make to our view of the daily food we eat and the daily drinks we drink knowing that bread and wine are sacramental? What difference does it make to our experience of water and soil and air, knowing that water is sacramental? . . . As Martin Luther wrote, "God writes the Gospel, not in the Bible alone, but also on trees and in the flowers and clouds and stars."

When we see all of life as sacramental, it changes our relationship to and our responsibility for creation. . . . We re-dedicate ourselves in worship to stop our actions that degrade nature and to find ways to restore God's creation."[3]

- Read the above passage through slowly a number of times, pausing to reflect on the questions within: What difference does it make for all our meals, knowing that the elements of our sacraments are food? How do the elements of the sacraments make a difference in how we encounter and belong in nature?
- "Listening" to creation as sacramental, how is the silence a part of a communion feast?
- Reflect on the fact that silence, too, is created. How does this affect how you listen to creation as sacramental?
- The "sound of silence" is a cliché. But how would you describe nature's sound of silence? In your experience, how does the Author of creation emerge from this silence?

3. The Web of Creation: www.webofcreation.org/Worship/reflection.htm (accessed September 2008).

CHAPTER EIGHT

Hovering and Hazelnuts as Contemplative Prayer

Hovering: Birds, Bees, Locusts, and a Fly

INTENTION   The intention of this practice is to attend to creatures that hover, noting their flight pattern as an aid to contemplation of nature.

PRACTICE   Watch a bird or insect that hovers, including various kinds of birds, bees, locusts, dragonflies, and the common housefly. Notice the intensity of activity that allows the creature to remain perfectly still. If it is not bee or locust or fly season, imagine a bird as it hovers.

- What does hovering allow the creature you are observing to be and to do?
- Imagine yourself and practice contemplation as hovering: centered and yet alert and conscious of the world around you. How would this affect your prayer, your image of God, your relationship to creation?
- Practice "hovering contemplation" from a number of perspectives:

1. Use contemplative hovering as a contemplative practice focused on objects of nature. For instance, contemplate a mountain in this way.
2. Allow objects or systems in creation to be themselves engaged in contemplative hovering. How do you perceive and experience a mountain as it "hovers" in this contemplative mode?
3. Imagine creation around you as the "hovering contemplation" of God. That is, the earth is in some sense a manifestation of God in contem-

plation, including you. How does God hover in contemplating a mountain into being? What do you notice about your contemplation of God and of nature?

4. Join creation in "hovering contemplation" of God. Here you are not necessarily praising God through creation; rather, with creation, your contemplation of God is intense stillness (wonder) in motion (attentiveness), noting the infinite manifestations of divine wisdom.

PRACTICE 8.2

Shells, Burrows, Nuts — Small Prayers and Large
[Full practice also in *Nature as Spiritual Practice*]

> If your heart is straight with God, then every creature will be to you a mirror of life and a book of holy doctrine. No creature is so little or so mean as not to show forth and represent the goodness of God.
> Thomas à Kempis, *Imitation of Christ*[1]

INTENTION Following Julian of Norwich and Thomas à Kempis, the intention of this practice is to embrace littleness in creation, and in doing so to embrace all that God is.

PRACTICE People love to collect objects from nature (and should, as long as collecting them will not harm or deplete the earth): shells, feathers, rocks and stones, coniferous cones, grasses, wildflowers, fragrant evergreen branches, sticks with interesting shapes, berries and leaves and flowers for arranging, plants for medicinal purposes. This is a finding, wondering, and perhaps even collecting practice.

- Find something — from some suggestions above — that draws your attention immediately. In creation, searching and finding are akin to attention and wonder.
- Hold this object: ideally, you will be able to cup it in the palm of your hand, as Julian does, but this is not essential. Meditate on this object. Explore it with all your senses, imagination, intellect, heart, and soul. How does it, as Thomas à Kempis says, "show forth and represent the goodness of God"?

1. Thomas à Kempis, *The Imitation of Christ*, ed. Harold Gardiner (Garden City, NY: Image, 1955), 80.

- Ask yourself why it exists, and why it exists with the particular characteristics it has. Ask yourself why it "is" rather than why it is "nought," as Julian says.
- Julian's answer is that God made, keeps, and loves it. Ask yourself the above question — why it "is" rather than why it is "nought" — in light of God's making, keeping, and loving it.
- Slowly let the object itself draw you to God.
- Julian marvels that a little thing, the hazelnut, is also in its own way "all that is made." That is, it is in microcosm representing the whole of all that is made — the macrocosm. Allow this "found" object to become a part of you and you a part of it. How are the two of you, together, a microcosm of "all that is made"?
- Take it home with you and live with it and it with you. What does it add to your prayer?

PRACTICE 8.3

Lessons in Prayer from a Small White Flower
[Full practice also in *Nature as Spiritual Practice*]

INTENTION   The intention of this practice is to place ourselves before nature with reverence, stillness, and openness in such a way that we absorb lessons from nature concerning our life of prayer and contemplation. These lessons may serve to reinforce and expand a current practice of prayer, or they may open completely new possibilities for prayer. We are going to attend to nature in a way similar to Jonathan Edwards's way. We will also be paying attention to how nature herself prays.

PRACTICE   Reread the passage from Jonathan Edwards on the small white flower in *Nature as Spiritual Practice.*
- Before beginning to observe nature, after you have reread the passage, spend some quiet time noting how Edwards uses the small white flower as a point of departure for distilling a host of formational spiritual practices. Some of these he was no doubt already familiar with; some the small white flower may have reframed in helpful ways; still others, we can only imagine, came to him as new ideas, perhaps even surprises in his prayerful conversation with the flower.
- In creation, begin "reading in nature" as a prayer in this way; observe,

be watchful for a comfortable place or a fine view or a single plant or animal that draws your attention.

- Notice all the ways in which the small white flower opens Edwards's heart and soul:
  - he says that he would like his soul to be like such a small white flower: low, humble, opening its bosom (his soul) to the intensity of the sun (God's love)
  - the small white flower is rejoicing
  - it is diffusing a sweet fragrance (for the Lord)
  - it is standing peacefully and lovingly in the midst of other small white flowers (faith community of souls)
  - as a creature, it is not in itself holy
  - it is calmly enraptured, lovely, humble, brokenhearted, with poverty of spirit
  - Edwards, as he meditates on the "stance" of the small white flower before God, wishes only that, in imitation of the flower, he might in the same way lie in the dust before God, with a panting heart, becoming as a small child.
- Remaining in place with your object or group of objects, begin to apply all senses (perhaps just one to begin, then begin adding as you feel the need). You may want to stand or sit close or at a distance. In whatever way you meditate, open your bosom (as Edwards would say) to whatever is calling you to be present.
- Begin to notice how what you've focused on maintains its relationship to the natural world around it. Is it small, large, colorful, broken, young, alone, supporting others, in a group, moving, at home on the earth, or at home in the sky, or on plants or trees? Give notice to anything that awakens your attention.
- It is obvious from Edwards's description that he is moving back and forth between the small white flower and what he knows as practice: the flower is small, low to the ground, humble; he has attempted the practice of humility before in a similar way, with mixed results. The flower seems to do it so gracefully and perfectly that nothing need be added or changed. The flower, in its way, is pure humility.
- Begin to associate what you notice in creation with a "posture" before God. As the associations come, at your own pace begin to associate these "postures" with spiritual-formation practices that you may already be familiar with but that the creation makes clear and explicit for you. Practice this posture; imitate it, consciously incorporating the pos-

ture into prayer. For instance, Edwards is put in mind of meekness, humility, broken-heartedness, and openness simply on the basis of observing a small white flower. What does nature put you in mind of in terms of reverence, prayer, or contemplation? Awakening to the spiritual and prayerful nature of creation in this way, imitate creation contemplation.

- The movement back and forth between Edwards and the small white flower involves a third: the Creator. The flower puts Edwards in mind of his own status measured against the Creator. The comparison leaves him wishing he could "lie down in the dust" before God, who is ALL. Take a bodily posture that represents your sense of God in the midst of this encounter with nature. If your meditation leads you to a desire to place all before the God of ALL by lying face-down flat on the ground, do so: it is prayer. If your urge is to touch or draw closer to the creation in acknowledgment of drawing closer to God, do so: it is prayer. Running, singing, twirling with arms in the air: it is prayer. Rage, tears, anger at what we do to this delicate but sustaining creation: it is prayer. Let your body pray as creation prays.
- Afterwards, you will want to spend some quiet time with this object or in this spot when you are finished, reflecting on what has transpired.
- As you leave, know that you are leaving with a greater sense of the possibilities of prayer and a greater appreciation for nature both as a teacher of prayer and as itself a prayer.
- Leave with thanksgiving.

PRACTICE 8.4

Visio Divina *(Sacred Seeing)*[2]

INTENTION   Based on the ancient practice of *lectio divina* (sacred reading), the intention of this practice is to select an image in nature that captures your gaze and to engage it in the prayer process of *visio divina* (sacred seeing).

PRACTICE   Take time to settle into a place where you will not be disturbed and where you can settle yourself into stillness. Get in touch with

2. This practice adapted from Christine Valters Painter, *Illuminating Mystery: Creativity as a Spiritual Practice* (Seattle: Abbey of the Arts Press, 2009), 3-6.

your breath and your body. Relish the silence. Be aware of this sacred time and become aware of your desire to draw closer to God.

1. *Gazing on nature. Lectio divina* is usually divided into four "moments." The first is the reading of God's Word; in *visio divina* we are dealing with a visual sacred text of creation. Begin by exploring as much of creation as you can; absorb it as you would sacred Scripture, but in this case absorb with your body, as well as mind and spirit. Allow your contemplative gaze to deepen as you begin to absorb subtleties in shadow and light, implication, and expression. Be aware of any particular aspect of the object that calls to you, challenges you, or invites you to deeper reflection.

2. *Reflecting on creation.* Allow the part of creation that captures your gaze to draw you more deeply into an experience of it. Allow it to unfold in your imagination, and notice if it evokes any memories, feelings, or other images. Create spaciousness within you to hold what is stirring. In *lectio divina,* this phase is typically referred to as meditation; in *visio divina,* this would mean becoming fully mindful of creation's presence and your experiences of it.

3. *Responding to creation.* After you have rested with this unfolding in your imagination in meditation, turn your focus to the ways you might want to respond to nature. How is God speaking to your life in this moment through creation, and how is the "yes" within that creation longing to be expressed? This phase of *lectio divina* is typically a phase of prayer; in the case of *visio divina,* this might involve conversations with God about what you have been "reading" and meditating on. Or it might involve prayerful conversation with creation. Take some time to reflect on your experience to this point by journaling or by becoming more fully aware of what the silence adds to your conversation.

4. *Resting in God.* After you have gotten in touch with the invitation extended to you by nature, simply rest in an awareness of God's loving presence through creation. This phase of *lectio divina* is typically the contemplative phase. Choose any contemplative practices you are familiar with, open yourself to creation, and simply rest. If you are not familiar with contemplative practices, this is a time to allow peace, rest, and calm to enter your relationship with creation; it is a time to allow yourself simply to be in trust and love with creation.

The Dark Night of the Planet

CHAPTER NINE

The Dark Night: Miseries and Signs

PRACTICE 9.1

In the Dark Night of the Planet
[Full practice also in *Nature as Spiritual Practice*]

INTENTION   The intention of this practice is to join the earth in darkness, in mourning.

PRACTICE
- What, in nature, have been your saddest experiences?
- What were the "natural" causes (i.e., causes from nature) of your anger, mourning, fear, or sadness?
- What have been human causes in nature of your personal despair or hopelessness or sadness?
- Reflect on the fact that Adam and Eve alone ate forbidden fruit, yet all creation suffers. What is most likely to arouse sorrow or mourning or loss in you as you experience or recall nature today?

Knowledge Is Change

INTENTION The intention of this practice is simply stated but a lifelong endeavor. It is to find out all you can about one ecological problem, imbalance, or crisis and respond to it.

PRACTICE Research, talk, attend seminars, join action groups, respond to one environmental issue that is important to you and to your community. If, for instance, it is global warming, find out how your community generates power; find out how transportation in your community is arranged; find out how other places on the globe affect your community; become informed about the "footprint" of your own energy consumption. Be informed about this issue, and begin by asking the hard questions.

- How does the information you gain affect your sense of presence to nature and nature's presence to you?
- How does the information you gain affect your spiritual journey, especially that part of your journey where you notice "ecological" and "sacramental" aspects of nature? What is the "sacramental" quality of environmental degradation?
- How does the information you gain affect your relationships with others, your family, your community, your church, yourself, and God?
- What is being done about this issue? What are the resistances to change? What can you do personally to effect positive change? How can you keep from becoming discouraged about a phenomenon that may at first seem insurmountable or beyond your ability to affect or control?
- You are not alone. Others are concerned about the very subject on which you are informing yourself. There is power in numbers. Having discerned the facts, how can you respond in a moral, responsible, and caring way to nature?

Nature Smart

INTENTION The intention of this practice is to add and apply "nature smarts," or naturalist intelligence, as suggested by Richard Louv, to Howard Gardner's original seven "smarts," or modes of intelligence. The intent is to apply this intelligence to nature (rather than human-made objects) and to affirm wonder as a crucial part of this intelligence.

PRACTICE Do the "Multiple Intelligence Inventory" in Appendix B in *Nature as Spiritual Practice* (based on the work of Howard Gardner). Regardless of how you score on the inventory, any of your natural "intelligences" can be turned toward creation. Gardner and Louv have since added the crucial eighth intelligence category, "naturalist intelligence." In the following practice, use your other "smarts" to help you exercise your newly emerging nature smarts.

- Notice how you use your "naturalist intelligence." In other words, what do you tend to notice in your environment? Do you mostly notice human-made objects, or do you mostly notice nature? What draws your attention, and to what do you then give your attention?
- Think of ways you could exercise your "naturalist intelligence" to become more nature smart. This exercise is equivalent to the spiritual practice of attention.
- Give yourself the opportunity to watch children at play or as they explore their world. Notice what they pay attention to with their "naturalist intelligence." Does it appear that their "naturalist intelligence" has already "been hijacked to deal with the world of man-made objects," as Gardner suggests, or are they using it to become nature smart?
- If you have children, or care for children in any way, what can you do to ensure that they apply their "naturalist intelligence" in a way that delights and communicates to them? In what ways can you help them sustain their nature smarts?
- Reflect on how wonder and curiosity contribute to "naturalist intelligence." In what ways have you lost this capacity to be astonished or to find wonder in nature? How might you recapture these in a sustained way?
- Pay very close attention to an animal or plant. Notice what "nature smarts" the animal or plant exhibits. How can you apply these "nature smarts" to your own life?

The Sounds of the Earth Crying[1]

[Full practice also in *Nature as Spiritual Practice*]

INTENTION The intention of this practice is to "hear the sounds of the earth crying," as Zen Buddhist monk Thich Nhat Hanh put it. In the process we allow our own pain for the earth to surface. Allowing our pain for the earth to surface is the healthy, nondenying response to ecological crisis.

PRACTICE This practice is best accomplished through small-group sharing, and I will describe it as a practice for a group. If you are not with a group, journal your responses and feelings. Do not be reluctant to acknowledge distress about the situation the planet is in; it is important in these exercises to express this uneasiness and distress. We are trying to encourage rather than discourage appropriate expression of feelings.

- If the group is new, make introductions. Let each participant have a period of time to explore thoughts and feelings about the environment without interruption.
- Have people gather in groups of about four (no fewer than three, no more than five). For this practice, allow each person his or her own period of time to speak, during which others listen without response. The time should be the same for all members (5-10 minutes), with a facilitator keeping track of time.
- If a speaker finishes early or pauses, the group should sit in silence until the period is up. Out of the silence, the speaker will often find more to say.
- Themes for sharing (limit the number to four or five) are open ended and general, focused on participants' pain for the earth (or how they "hear the earth crying"). It is helpful to post themes on PowerPoint or in a handout. Possible themes for discussion might include:
  - A recent experience of the condition of the planet
  - When earth-suffering or uncertainty has impinged on your life
  - Time you felt pain for creation particularly acutely
  - When you first noticed you felt pain for the earth

1. Joanna Macy and Molly Young Brown, *Coming Back to Life: Practices to Reconnect Our Lives, Our World* (Gabriola Island, BC: New Society Publishers, 1998), 27. The outline for this practice is found on pp. 91-94.

   – How your feelings of pain for the earth have evolved
   – What concerns you most about the earth today is . . .
   – What you think the condition of our environment is becoming . . .
   – Ways you avoid these feelings are . . .
- After all have had a chance to speak without interruption, let the small groups as a whole share experiences and feelings for fifteen minutes. This portion of small-group discussion can center on issues that arose during the uninterrupted time, or any issues the group would like to explore.
- Reconvene the entire group and discuss themes and experiences that arose. Though solutions or inclinations toward action may be a part of this discussion, try to stay with earth sadness, the "earth crying," for this practice.
- If you are journaling, do the same. If it is easier for you to write your feelings as a letter to a friend, or as a letter to God, do so. Again, honor your feelings of pain for the planet and give yourself permission to express them.

PRACTICE 9.5

Practice in a World of Decay, Violence, and Death

INTENTION The intention of this practice is to begin thinking about and experiencing decay, violence, and death in the natural world as spiritual practice, formative of Christian identity in the dark night.

PRACTICE Most people today try to separate themselves from or ignore violence and death in the natural world. Though scientists cannot prove that nonhuman animals enjoy living, we can, as Alexander Skutch writes, "seek indications and weigh possibilities" that they do. What does this mean for the harsh violence repeated on earth millions of times every moment of the day? Christian spiritual formation is concerned with just such "indications" and "possibilities."

- Recall the most unsettling death in the natural world you can remember. Or as you sit, walk, and work in nature, "seek indications" and "weigh possibilities" of violence and death that you can find today. Once you start looking, you will see them all around.

- With the death of each grebe, each baby baboon, housefly, or leaf, something sacramental is gone. How do you fit this sacramental loss into your "Christian" perspective?
- If you were to speak to God about the death you witness, experience, or remember, how would you frame the conversation?
- Please, do speak to or be in communication with God through prayer and meditation about this very question. Do not be afraid to be angry about the cruelty you've seen. You will not offend God; apparently, God is not afraid.
- Become aware of harmony and conflict in nature. What is the transition point or "contact boundary" between the realities of harmony and conflict in the natural world. How does the movement between the two fit into your experience of the Christian life?
- Alexander Skutch says: "If all nonhuman creatures are devoid of the psychic attributes called anthropomorphic, it follows that during the immense age before humans arose, no gleam of joy, no warmth of affection, nothing to give living intrinsic value brightened the expanse of any of the myriad animals that swarmed over a hospitable planet."[2] Use this as a thought experiment to imagine a world swarming with life but without joy, affection, or "brightening." Can you picture such a world? Do you think that is how it was? Or was some joy and affection present even from the beginning?
- Reflect on the degraded areas of the planet that today experience "no gleam of joy, no warmth of affection, nothing to give living intrinsic value."

PRACTICE 9.6

The Giving Tree

INTENTION The intention of this practice is to meditate, using Scripture, *lectio divina,* and nature, on humanity's long history of indifferent stewardship of creation, humanity's apparent denial of creation-pain, and to ask what this long history might mean for us today.

PRACTICE Take your Bible and find a quiet spot in a forest. If there are few forests in your area, a city park or a grove of trees will serve you

---

2. Alexander F. Skutch, *Harmony and Conflict in the Living World* (Norman: University of Oklahoma Press, 2000), 133.

well. Try to find a spot where you can sit and not be disturbed. Before reading the suggested Scripture passage, spend a good amount of time reading the book of the forest. Let the forest soak into you and you into the forest. Be conscious of this simple time of attention, listening, and participating as a time of prayer. Tune yourself to the grammar of the trees.

- Very slowly, read either Psalm 104 or the second creation account through the eating of the fruit (Gen. 2:4b–3:7). As you read, do so in the context of your understanding of ecological crisis or environmental stress. You will be paying particular attention to the obvious discontinuity between creation's grammar in Scripture and creation's current grammar of pain. For example, in Psalm 104:10-12, linger over the springs that "gush forth from the valleys, flow between mountains." Do they "gush forth" today? If they do, are they drinkable? Are they fitting habitations for the birds of the air, as the psalm says?
- As you read slowly, stop from time to time to be watchful, to attend to, to touch, smell, and hear something of creation around you that is mentioned in Scripture. This is actually one vital form of *lectio divina* (sacred reading): *lectio* (reading), meditation (applying your senses, imagination, feelings, and thoughts to creation), prayer (conversing verbally with God and nature), and contemplation (simply resting in and becoming a part of the forest or ecology around you).
- Another example is the following: stop at Genesis 2:7, pick up some dust, dirt, or soil from the ground, and examine it, sense it, pray over it. Form the soil (or simply hold it in your hand if it does not naturally cohere) and breathe your own breath into the form, giving it "the breath of life." Imagine God "breathing" into this humble dirt, and into everything around you. Imagine how every living thing inhales just such a divine breath in rhythm with you.
- What is the relationship between the purity of divine breath and what we have in fact done to the sacred air, wind, and atmosphere that envelops us?
- Reread this same verse, substituting "I" or "me" for "man," and "my" for "his."
- After reflecting on the above, turn your attention to a careful rereading of Genesis 3:1-6 about the serpent, the tree of the knowledge of good and evil, and Adam and Eve. Find a tree around you to be your "tree of the knowledge of good and evil."

- Think of all the things that could have possibly tempted Adam and Eve to eat the fruit. Obviously, the serpent is culpable; but for any number of reasons, Adam and Eve are culpable as well. What convinced them to eat? What was the longing or need that drove them?
- Turn your attention back to the tree near you. Ask whether this tree of the knowledge of good and evil is in any way culpable. What was the tree's "role" in the Fall? We can say, at the least, that the tree was doing what a tree was meant to do — offering a gift of fruit.

PRACTICE 9.7

Trees and Birds Never Born
[Full practice also in *Nature as Spiritual Practice*]

INTENTION   One astute writer has observed that what is saddest about the extinction of species — the word "extinction" itself constricts the throat — is that never again will any individual of that extinct species be born. The intention of this practice is to recognize that the eradication of a species of bird or tree is the eradication of birth and of new life as well.

PRACTICE   For this practice you will have to do your own exploring. It can be carried out in one (or both) of two ways. First, however, reread the two tender paragraphs by Peattie in *Nature as Spiritual Practice*. Then —

1. If you have a special connection with a species that has recently become extinct, concentrate the practice on one or a small number of individuals of this species. If you cannot think of one, do some research to find a species of tree or bird or fish or mammal that is either extinct or highly endangered due to human exploitation.
   - Find out all you can about the species in order to know everything that it contributed and everything that has now been lost. Stay with this species for several days or weeks, holding it in prayer and meditation, as if it were a guide to your own sadness. How does it guide you? Where is it now?
   - Notice what, in nature, the absence of this species means to creation. What do you expect this loss means to God?
   - As you go about your day, or as you are able to be with nature, try to imagine the rebirth of that species. What would it look like? How would it affect its ecosystem? Notice how you feel about the fact

that another member of this species will never again be born. Whatever feelings arise in you — sadness, sorrow, loss, grief, pain, fear, anxiety, anger — let these be prayer.

2. In the second way, walk or sit or work in the natural world until you see an individual of a species of bird or tree that may be numerous and that you have been very attached to over the years.

   - Imagine that the individual to whom you are turning your attention is a member of a species that is becoming extinct. Now imagine that this individual to which you are giving attention is the last member of this species of creation — and that this individual, after a time, also dies. What of the "sacramental" vanishes with this extinction?

   - As above, note how you feel; do not censor yourself. Journal or simply note what emerges and let your feelings come. With the absence of this species that has been so meaningful to you over the years, how do you feel? What does it mean to you that another will never be born? How can you pray this loss? How do you feel about the natural world in general?

CHAPTER TEN

Darkness: Consenting to Creative Love

Nature Lament[1]

INTENTION   The intention of this practice is to enter the dark night of the planet truthfully and honestly by writing a nature lament.

PRACTICE: WRITING YOUR OWN LAMENT   Writing our own laments takes us more deeply into our own pain. It also gives us some cathartic release from that pain, as we acknowledge the pain and present it to God. Laments can even encompass the most paradoxical component of darkness: the wound of love. You may do the writing for this practice anywhere. You will need writing materials and a Bible, or at least a copy of Psalm 71.

Read and reflect on the following short outline of a lament psalm and the notes on the importance and power of lament. The outline uses Psalm 71 as an example, so you will want to read each portion of Psalm 71 as it is keyed to the outline below. The outline provides traditional aspects of a lament and a few suggestions in brackets to focus the lament on creation. After you have read through Psalm 71 and the outline, write your own lament for the dark night of the planet. Use as many or as few of the "forms" of a lament that are outlined as you want. Do not hold anything back in the

1. Adapted from Kathleen D. Billman and Daniel L. Migliore, *Rachel's Cry: Prayer of Lament and Rebirth of Hope* (Eugene, OR: Wipf and Stock, 2007).

writing. When you have finished the writing, read the lament and reflect on the experience of writing it. If you feel comfortable, share it with another person.

- You may choose to write the lament from your perspective as one who is responsible for some aspect of the dark night of the planet (a penitential lament), or you may want to write from the perspective of creation itself in lament, or from a perspective in which you join creation in lament.

The Formfulness of Lament

Psalms of lament, both individual and communal, can be distinguished from psalms that express thanksgiving and praise, penitence, trust, or wisdom. They have a characteristic structure or form:

1. *Address to God.* The address to God is usually a brief cry for help, but it is occasionally expanded to include a statement of praise or a recollection of God's intervention (in creation) in the past (Ps. 71:1-3).
2. *Complaint.* The lamenter informs God of diverse problems or concerns that individuals or a community (or creation) experience. In penitential psalms, the complaint can be the acknowledgment of one's sins (toward the planet) (Ps. 71:4).
3. *Confession of trust.* The psalmist remains confident in God despite the circumstances and begins to see his or her (or the planet's) problems differently (Ps. 71:5-8).
4. *Petition.* Having expressed confidence in God, the psalmist appeals to God for deliverance and intervention (for the planet). The petitioner might express reasons why God should intervene, ranging from the petitioner's confession of despair in the midst of God's faithfulness to God's act of creation in the past (Ps. 71:9-13).
5. *Words of assurance.* The psalmist expresses certainty that the petition will be heard by God (creation) (Ps. 71:14a).
6. *Vow of praise.* The lament concludes with the psalmist's vow to witness to God's intervention (in creation) (Ps. 71:14b-24).
7. *Earth care.* Not usually associated with lament psalms, but you may wish to "covenant" a new way of belonging to creation.

The Importance and Power of Lament
- It is a transcending form of discourse, moving beyond the current reality.
- It acknowledges the limitations of an embodied life.
- It confirms the value of an embodied life.

- It grants permission to grieve and protest.
- It empowers someone when he or she feels vulnerable.
- It prepares the way for new understandings of God.
- It strengthens our self-understanding as responsible agents.
- It purifies anger and the desire for vengeance.
- It promotes solidarity with those who suffer.
- It revitalizes praise and hope.

PRACTICE 10.2

Miseries in This Earth's Dark Night

INTENTION   The intention of this practice is to confirm in our minds and hearts the reality of the dark night of the planet and to intentionally acknowledge our part in precipitating or maintaining the planet's miseries. We will acknowledge and affirm about our planet, with our own eyes, what Saint John of the Cross confirms about the human soul.

PRACTICE   Become familiar with the three "miseries of the earth" as described by Saint John of the Cross, in *Nature as Spiritual Practice.*

- Each time you engage in this practice, allow yourself to be drawn to a place in creation that captures your attention. By now you know how to see creation with attentive wonder. The earth is the recipient of divine, inflowing love. Notice inflowing love, but then begin to notice with "God's eyes" the "miseries of the earth" that are perversions of this love.
- As a symbol of your intention to acknowledge and affirm the dark night of the planet, gently touch something of the earth as a prayer of centering and mindfulness, and acknowledge divine love for this object. Return to this object as needed to maintain your center.
- Take some time to imagine the planet, in its dark night, to be blinded by the pure brilliance of the divine light and prevented from "seeing" by each of the miseries described in the text.
- Take seriously the invitation in Job 12:7-8 to ask the earth itself about the qualities of each misery. Ask creation and listen to creation.
- How is God present or absent in creation through each of these miseries? How do they contribute to the planet's dark night?
- Sit or walk and journal or photograph the planet in its darkness. What

other miseries do you experience of the earth's dark night? Can you be a "companion of consolation" to the earth in these miseries?

- How can you best communicate these miseries of the earth to another human?
- For Saint John of the Cross, a dark night — though it seems otherwise — is a movement toward transformation. But transformation does not happen in a vacuum. How can you contribute to the earth's transformation from the darkness you experience?

PRACTICE 10.3

Signs of the Dark Night of the Planet

INTENTION   The intention of this practice is to listen to the earth, hearing in her sighs and groans the three signs of the dark night described by Saint John of the Cross.

PRACTICE   As everyone hears creation's praise in different ways, so too do we hear and see the symptoms of the dark night of the planet in different ways. Use your own imagination, creativity, patience, and humility to experience the symptoms of the dark night of the planet. Again, you may wish to journal, photograph, or draw what you experience — or simply observe. Keep in mind that we are not disconnected from nature; we are all a part of nature's dark night.

- First, find some thing or some spot in nature that you feel *is* praising God.
- Then leave this place or object and begin to give attentive devotion to places or activities in creation that show signs of the dark night of the planet. To do this, first notice how the earth no longer finds consolation in the things of God (you will need to notice initially how and where the earth *does* find consolation). How do you witness how creation gets cut off from this consolation?
- Second, how does the earth, even in the midst of this desolation, still long for God? To help your precision as you carefully note how the earth does or does not continue to reach out to its Creator, write down your observations or make photographs or write about them in letter form to a friend — or even to God.
- There are many instances in Scripture and from the church's tradition that refer to the earth's prayer, meditation, or contemplative adora-

tion of the Lord. To witness the third sign, spend time in Scripture as you note how the earth, even when not explicitly described as such, nonetheless has a natural longing for connection and belonging to God. Then spend time in creation joining the earth as it longs for connectivity through its natural inclination to pray, meditate, contemplate, and praise the Creator. Pray with the mountain, pray with the lion, pray with Queen Anne's lace from the midst of this longing. Notice where and how the earth fails to make the connection of praise it longs to make. What is blocking creation from the divine connection it longs for?

- What are ways you are connected to the earth that might be blocking its natural longing to "return to the Creator"? How might you maintain connection with the earth in ways that enhance earth's longing and capacity for connection with the Creator?

PRACTICE 10.4

The Way of All Earth?
[Full practice also in *Nature as Spiritual Practice*]

INTENTION One study from the Union of Concerned Scientists lists the "leading consumption-related environmental problems" today as:

- Air pollution
- Global warming
- Habitat alteration
- Water pollution

The same study lists the "most harmful consumer activities" as:

- Cars and light trucks
- Meat and poultry
- Home heating, hot water, and air conditioning
- Household appliances and lighting
- Home construction
- Household water and sewage[2]

2. Michael Brower and Warren Leon, *The Consumer's Guide to Effective Environmental Choices: Practical Advice from the Union of Concerned Scientists* (New York: Three Rivers Press, 1999).

The intention of this practice is to consider whether this dark night of the planet is a transformational phase or permanent condition. Explore your own reactions to this phase and/or condition.

PRACTICE   Perhaps the most pessimistic (or realistic, depending on perspective and circumstances) portrayal of life, death, and the afterlife in all of Scripture comes from Ecclesiastes 9:1-10. Koheleth, the sage of Ecclesiastes, says that regardless of what we do in this life, we will never understand the meaning of life or death, let alone escape the grasp of death. For Koheleth, human life is a wisp of straw: there is no moral justice in the destiny of men or women; it is vanity to think that there is any sacredness or dignity in human life. The writer concludes that one should enjoy pleasures as they come, because regardless of what we do, "the same fate comes to all" (Eccles. 9:2).

- Read Ecclesiastes 9:1-10.
- What is transformational in this passage?
- Read the passage again. This time apply what is said of humanity to creation. That is, bring to mind the reality that all creation meets the same fate as humanity as it is depicted in these verses.
- From this perspective, do you feel the earth is in a transformational phase, or do you feel this dark night of the planet may be a permanent condition, experiencing "the same fate [that] comes to all"?
- How does this perspective affect your own sense of who you are? What does it mean for your relationship with nature? What insight does it shed on your own experience of the dark night?
- Imagine both possibilities. What can or should we do about the dark night of the planet if this is a transformational phase? On the other hand, imagine possible responses if this dark night is a permanent condition.
- Imagine that Saint Francis of Assisi is there beside you. What would he tell you? What would you like to tell him about the dark night?

PRACTICE 10.5

Consenting to Creative Love
[Full practice also in *Nature as Spiritual Practice*]

> Listen, O heavens, and I will speak;
>> hear, O earth, the words of my mouth.
> Let my teaching fall like rain
>> and my words descend like dew,
> like showers on new grass,
>> like abundant rain on tender plants.

Deuteronomy 32:1-2

INTENTION   The intention of this practice is to consent to hear Love speak through nature's consent to be exactly what it is, according to the divine intention.

PRACTICE   In this practice, use the three excerpts cited in the text — Job 12:7-8, the Merton tree quote, and Deuteronomy 32:1-2 — separately or together as you move through the exercise.

- Following Merton, notice how something in nature gives glory to God simply by being itself. In what ways do you notice nature "consenting" to be itself? Consenting to creative love is a vocation as well as a core of prayer. True consent of this kind structures and shapes us for maximum engagement and flourishing for the life given us. True consent in this sense unites us to our Creator. Look again at what you are attending to in nature — a wave or a tree or a red-tailed hawk — and simply notice how readily it consents to be itself, and in this consenting is in fact a deeply sacred form of prayer.
- The Job passage invites us to learn about consenting, vocation, and prayer from nature. Ask the animals, the plants, the mountains what you need to know about consenting to creative love, about your vocation, and about prayer. Give your sacred attention to how nature answers and "declares" to you. The context of the Job passage is that the animals will declare that God is their maker. In your own context, what do nature's answers teach you about God? Ask the animals about how they manage to be themselves in the dark night of the planet.
- From a slightly different perspective, the Deuteronomy passage indicates that nature herself learns from the wisdom of God. How/what do the heavens hear when God speaks? How does the earth listen and

learn when creative love opens its mouth? How do the Lord's teachings fall like rain, like dew on the grass and plants? How do these ways of listening and learning form your own senses to listen to and learn from God and nature?

- What are you doing in your life that prevents a tree, a wave, or any part of nature from "consenting" to what God is calling it to be? Expressed another way, what kind of "footprint" do you leave on the earth that contributes to the dark night?

PRACTICE 10.6

Belonging and Anger

INTENTION   The intention of this practice is threefold: first, to observe feelings and connections associated with belonging within creation; second, to allow transgression of belonging in the natural world to evoke anger as virulent as Jesus' anger in the temple; and third, to question whether both belonging and anger are appropriate ways of participating in ecological and sacred creation.

PRACTICE   Several years ago, at a Jesuit retreat house, I encountered what I now believe to be a holy man. He gave me a word. The man was a very old Jesuit priest and my spiritual director during my time at the retreat house. I was dubious when I first met him. I was concerned not so much about his age per se — I find wisdom in ancient places — but rather about his apparent inability to follow a line of thought or conversation. In a word, I thought he was probably becoming senile. It turned out that, instead, it was I who had a youthful version of senility. After I had spent a number of very frustrating sessions with him, he opened his mouth and spoke a word that was to become brilliant in its simple clarity. He spoke very briefly about the humanity of Jesus and how through Jesus' humanity we are — all of us — humanity and creation, connected as family. (I remember that the appropriateness of this little speech eluded me at the time.) Then he stopped, was silent for a time, giving his face fully to mine, and finally he simply said, "You should think about belonging." He didn't say much more over the course of my time there; but in that phrase he said everything. Throughout the rest of the retreat, "belonging" became a byword of the holy: belonging to others, belonging to myself, belonging to God, but especially belonging to creation.

- Slowly reread several times — and absorb the details in — Matthew 21:12-13 (printed in the text) about the money changers in the temple and Jesus' reaction to them.
- Now spend time in nature, journaling about or photographing what you experience as "belonging" in the natural world. However you attend to nature, what constitutes "belonging" in nature to you?
- You might notice how the honeybee "belongs" to a field of flowers, how the raptor belongs as a predator, how a river belongs to a countryside and the countryside to a river, how green belongs to grass.
- How do earth, wind, fire, and water belong together in the organic, sacred ecology of nature?
- Where do you belong in this setting? You may want to start with connections you are familiar with that give you a sense of belonging, such as families or other communities, and then "shift" that sense of belonging to creation. How are you part of a community of belonging with nature?
- We have spoken of and practiced nature as a kind of temple; we have certainly explored nature as a house of prayer. What is the quality and intensity of your sense of belonging to nature as a house of prayer?
- Notice now, or over the next few days, if you can find something that humanity has done to disturb this balance of belonging and connection in nature. How are you implicated in this disturbance as a sacred, belonging member of humanity?
- When the sellers and money changers violated the web of belonging in the temple, Jesus became very angry. He reacted immediately and did not apologize for his "destruction" or the "interruption" of commerce that had itself destroyed the sacred belonging that the temple was intended to ordain.
- Scripture and tradition invite us to share a sense of belonging with nature. Commerce that uses up nature only for the sake of profit is not a form of belonging: it is manipulation, degradation, and ultimately destruction of both belonging and of ecology.
- How can you become angry about this loss of belonging and ecology? How can you, in the imagery of Matthew 21, overturn tables and throw money changers and merchants out of the temple of nature?
- This practice is an invitation to become as angry as you possibly can — just as angry as Jesus was in the temple. Jesus was *destructive*, but only with the goal of restoring *constructive* balance and belonging within his Father's house of prayer. If it helps, imagine and imitate how Jesus felt his anger and how he acted on the basis of his anger.

- Can you remain "disturbed," yet still "curious" enough to investigate and address with wisdom the source of your anger?

PRACTICE 10.7

Creation Confession

INTENTION The philosopher Roger S. Gottlieb has recently written: "People have always had moral failings, but they have never had to confess to devastating creation, or felt the need to pray for the health of the earth as an endangered whole." The intention of this practice is to help us find our own personal (or communal) languages for confessing our contribution to the dark night of the planet, to ask forgiveness, and to pray for the health of the earth.

PRACTICE For Earth Day, April 21, 2002, the Ecojustice Task Force of the National Council of Churches sent a packet of worship materials to each of the NCC's 170,000 member congregations. The packet included the following "Prayer of Confession." Read through, pray, and meditate on this confession. Add your own confession of your part in "devastating creation."

> On this Earth Sabbath, we open our minds to learn about ecological threats to the health of present and future generations and to the whole community of life.
>
> We reach out our hands to bring healing and change, for the sake of the children of the earth — past, present, and future.
>
> The prophets Isaiah and Hosea said: The land lies polluted under its inhabitants. The beasts of the field, the birds of the air, even the fish of the sea are dying.
>
> God of mercy, we confess that we are damaging the earth, the home that you have given us. We buy and use products that pollute our air, land, and water, harming wildlife and endangering human health.
>
> Forgive us, O God, and inspire us to change.
>
> Chief Seattle said: Whatever we do to the web of life we do to ourselves.
>
> God of justice, we confess that we have not done enough to protect the web of life. We have failed to insist that our government set standards based on precaution. We allow companies to release

dangerous toxins that destroy fragile ecosystems and harm human beings, especially those among us who are most vulnerable.

We are connected with those who have gone before us: the martyrs and heroes, all the ancestors who invested themselves for the sake of future generations, and we are connected with those who will come after us.

Our ancestors and descendants support us — we are their champions.

We are related to the earth and all its creatures in a web that cannot be broken without injury to all.

The earth and our fellow creatures support us — we are their advocates. We are connected to Jesus Christ, who reveals God to us, sends us the Spirit, and sends us out in his name.[3]

- What in this confession speaks and gives language to your own personal (or your community's) "moral failings"? Why? Be honest with yourself and with God. Focus first on yourself, then on your local community, then open into expanding concentric circles of communities to which you belong, including ecological communities.
- Express your moral failings against creation as a prayer of confession.
- Pray your prayer of confession, preferably directly to and in the presence of that part of God's creation you have identified as being degraded because of your action or inaction. Allow creation to be a part of the prayer as you ask forgiveness.
- Journal or talk with a spiritual friend about your confessional prayer, your experience in praying it, and how you can pray together for the health of the earth.
- Just as memory and honesty are preparations for confession, so too is our own human response to the details of the confession in concert with the Spirit's guidance. True confession actually consists of memory, confession as prayer, and response. Take the action your prayers guide you toward. Sense that this action is also a part of your prayer of confession.
- As part of your prayer, envision an earth healed and healthy. Continue to know that your response is part of your prayer of confession and your path to forgiveness.

3. National Council of Churches, Ecojustice Task Force: http://www.nccecojustice.org/EarthDay/2002/index.html (accessed Oct. 10, 2007).

Nature as Spiritual Guide

CHAPTER ELEVEN

Nature as Belonging

Balance in Discernment
[Full practice also in *Nature as Spiritual Practice*]

INTENTION   Balance is critical to discernment. The intention of this practice is to recognize balance and imbalance in nature and how you walk with balance or imbalance in nature.

PRACTICE   In his book *Drawing Closer to Nature,* the artist Peter London teaches how to pay careful attention to the natural world, in effect how to separate, sift, and decide — how to discern.[1] The book gives practices in both drawing (pictorially) closer to nature and drawing (attentively) closer to nature. Allow yourself at least an hour of uninterrupted time for this practice.

- Find a place in nature where you are comfortable and where you can spend time exploring the subtle balances and imbalances in creation. Breathe, be still.
- When you are ready, begin going through the list of "balances" below. The idea is to recognize a statement that begins "Balance is . . ." in the natural world around you. Move from one to the next only as you feel

1. Peter London, *Drawing Closer to Nature: Making Art in Dialogue with the Natural World* (Boston: Shambala, 2003). For a discussion of balance and most of the balance suggestions, see pp. 210ff.

the need or as the next catches your attention. Focus on whatever draws your attention: a tree, the ecosystem, colors, a few blades of grass, wind, waves.

- Notice these balances in nature, then do an internal accounting of how you are yourself balanced or imbalanced in a similar way. This internal accounting or "examen of conscious" is a preliminary step in discernment.
- How does nature guide your contemplations and meditations in directions that help you live mindfully, that is, how you walk the earth in balance? Again, you may wish to journal, draw, photograph, or "track," from your field guide, your particular nature interest — birding, for instance. Whatever helps you pay careful attention to nature will help you focus on balance in nature.

"Balances":
- Balance is to locate the still point at the center of complexity.
- Balance is to be in a constant state of sensitive fine adjustments.
- Balance requires exquisite sensitivity to inner and outer forces.
- Balance requires yielding and resisting, yielding and resisting.
- Balance appears spontaneous and improvisational, but is utterly responsible and devoted.
- Balance is thwarted by pretense, also by insistence.
- Balance knows both this and that, and prefers neither.
- Balance is opportunistic.
- Balance finds home anywhere, finds the center everywhere.
- "Balancing" is more in balance than "balanced."
- Complete balance is the end of nature.

PRACTICE 11.2

Slowing

INTENTION In his book *In Praise of Slowness: Challenging the Cult of Speed,* Carl Honoré writes of the ever-increasing speed of contemporary life. He writes: "In this media-drenched, data-rich, channel-surfing, computer-gaming age, we have lost the art of doing nothing . . . of slowing down and simply being alone with our thoughts." He quotes the actress Carrie

Fisher, who said that "even instant gratification takes too long."[2] Belonging to nature is a process of slowing, of being willing to pay attention to a periwinkle or linger with a cloud. The intention of this practice is to begin to restore contemplative connection with creation by slowing down.

PRACTICE Recall and reread the quote from Thomas Merton introduced in the previous chapter that begins, "A tree gives glory to God by being a tree."

- Notice how creation "consents" to God's creative love by being itself. We, like the tree, can also consent to God's creative love by slowing and by simply being ourselves. In the power of the slowing we again begin to belong to creation.
- This practice can be done in solitude or with a group. If you are in a group, form a circle; if you are alone, walk as described in solitude. Walk meditatively and in time with your breathing. As you inhale, take one step. Allow the step to coincide with the time it takes to inhale. As you exhale, take another short step in the same way. Walk in a circle with others (or in solitude) at this slow pace of your breathing.
- Allow the group to break up and, continuing this slow pace, spend time tuned to nature, watching and noticing how all creation, simply by being itself, gives glory to God. You may find yourself giving attention to a single object or even an attribute (such as "green") or to the open functioning of an ecological system.
- Continue walking slowly — in time with your breath. Begin to notice and experience how all things in nature consent in obedience to God's creative love, to be just what they are. Notice plants, animals, birds, insects: they all move, are shaped and colored, and behave in a way that makes it impossible for them to do or be in any other way than they are.
- Spend time in small groups discussing or journaling how, by "slowing," you can consent to this creative love in the same way, and how this consent bonds you with nature.

---

2. Carl Honoré, *In Praise of Slowness: Challenging the Cult of Speed* (New York: Harper-One, 2004), 11, 12.

Clouds of Discernment

INTENTION The intention of this practice is to continue to recognize and experience nature as guide in discernment and healing by noticing consolations and desolations in nature.

PRACTICE By taking an internal accounting, we discern that nature teaches healing. Healing nature is closely related to healing ourselves.

- Look closely at clouds. As in the story of Vermeer and Griet, spend time with the clouds in intimate, slow attending. Notice the colors you see in the cloud. Do not be satisfied with just "white" or "gray."
- Freeman House describes nature as many sets of eyes staring out from the same living body. How might you describe how the cloud sees you or what the cloud communicates to you? Consider how you think Jesus might have experienced this very cloud.
- Discernment as internal accounting happens in many ways. One way is to note consolations: things or events that (1) capture your attention, (2) seem true, and (3) bring delight or a sense of well-being. Discernment also happens when we notice and attend to desolations: events that capture our attention and may seem true, but our feelings or experiences are opposite to those of consolation.

  1. As you observe the cloud, do you experience consolations or desolations?
  2. Noticing your "inner guidance system," how do you "belong together" with the cloud and with the cloud's environment?
  3. What in your life is currently a matter for discernment? Notice consolation and desolation and whatever connects you through nature to this matter for discernment.
  4. In what direction has this discernment process in nature moved you — toward or away from God?

- Discernment is as much about confirmation by others who know you well as it is about internal movements of consolation and desolation. Tell someone you trust as much as you can about this encounter and what it means to you. What is that person's response?
- Reflect on how you can experience nature as a discerning guide in a habitual way.

Vocation, Discernment, and Healing

INTENTION Our "vocation" is our listening for, hearing, and response to God's call. The intention of this practice is to discern God's intimate and healing call as it is spoken to us through nature.

PRACTICE Discerning vocation is itself a spiritual art or practice: it requires careful attention while remaining open to the influences of the Spirit.

- Each of the guidelines below can be used in nature as a way in which to listen for, hear, and respond in discernment to the *vocatio* of God.
- Take your journal and move into a part of the natural world that awakens a sense of intimacy. As you are moving into the natural world, walking, watching, and listening, pray with God about what you are doing and why you are here. Pray your longing to hear God's voice through nature.
- When you have settled on a location, sit down and just listen and watch for a time. Then make a list:
  - Things in nature that nurture your mind, body, or spirit
  - Positive aspects of your life as you experience them in the natural world
  - Don't censor yourself. As you work, this is your unconscious nature-vocation, your nature-passion. You are simply allowing nature to assist in making conscious those things that connect with your deepest longings.
- Divide the list into the following categories: Seeking God; Work; Study; Spiritual Community and Worship; Care of Our Bodies; Service to Others; Hospitality; Transformation. Note the relative number of activities in each category; some may have many, some none.
- How is God calling you through nature's voice in each of these activities?
  - Would you like to find a different balance within each of the categories?
  - What you have listed are your passions. Reflect on how you can practice being intentional about dedicating each of the activities you are passionate about to God.
  - What are your gifts, and how do they align with the activities you

listed? Your gifts and longings help you hear God speaking through nature.

- How comfortable are you with the values and ideas you have been embracing for the last several years? Do they conform to what you believe to be your true self as you experience it in nature?

- Once again, set your initial list and their categories in the context of the natural world. If they are in harmony with the natural world, your list may be truly indicative of your own vocation. On the other hand, they may seem to be a little "off kilter" or "out of balance" with the truth in nature you see and experience around you. Spend some time reflecting on why they fit or do not fit.

• After spending time reflecting and writing, leave with gratitude for what nature has contributed to discerning and keeping your vocation.

• A follow-up to this practice is to shape what you have discerned into a "rule of life": in other words, how can you best exercise the passions and desires of your heart that you have learned of in nature. The "rule" can be anything from a schedule for doing those things you enjoy and/ or feel the need to do to restore balance in nature, to particular practices you devise for yourself to exercise those same passions and desires. Do not be hard on yourself: make your "rule of life" practicable, and take small steps at first.

CHAPTER TWELVE

Nature as Healing and Solace

PRACTICE 12.1

Suffering into Song
[Full practice also in *Nature as Spiritual Practice*]

INTENTION   The intention of this practice is, through a process of mutual invitation, to encourage transformational healing through nature by turning suffering into song.

PRACTICE   This is a group process, developed by Eric Law, a consultant on multicultural leadership. I envision it here as a practice that invites turning "suffering into song."[1]

- A facilitator provides the group with the following three questions to discuss, introduced one at a time:
    1. What is the deepest suffering or loss you have experienced in nature?
    2. What have you learned since then that speaks to this suffering or loss?
    3. How do you understand God's presence or absence in this suffering or loss?

---

1. The questions have been altered, but this practice otherwise follows a detailed description of Law's "mutual invitation" group processes in Jaco J. Hamman, "Remembering the Dismembered: Teaching for Transformation and Restoration," *The Journal of Pastoral Theology* 16, no. 1 (Spring 2006): 44-59.

- The facilitator explains the process of "mutual invitation" as follows: one member of the group is appointed "leader" by the facilitator and empowered to lead off by answering the first question. For each question, sharing is limited to two minutes for each person. When finished, the person sharing invites another person to speak.
- All those invited to share have three options:

  1. They can share for two minutes, answering the question under discussion.
  2. They can say "Pass for now" if they need more time to reflect.
  3. They can say "Pass" if they don't want to say anything at all about the specific question under discussion.

- After the leader has spoken, she or he invites a fellow group member (not necessarily the person sitting next to her or him) to share: "I invite [person's name] to share." The leader functions as the timekeeper for the group.
- The second person either answers the question or responds with "Pass" or "Pass for now" and invites another group member to share.
- The process continues with the first question until every member has had a chance to respond.
- The leader addresses the next question and follows the same procedure.
- After all three questions have been addressed, allow time for open, honest, and nonjudgmental discussion.

PRACTICE 12.2

The Healing Embrace of Green

INTENTION To experience the healing embrace of green (Hildegard's *viriditas*, the vital source and will to life of nature) and to pray the green.

PRACTICE If you are in a group, discuss:

1. What does Hildegard of Bingen mean by *viriditas*?
2. What are the similarities and differences between Jesus Christ in the world, the Holy Spirit in the world, and *viriditas*?
3. Compare the human soul, as it is a part of the human person, and *viriditas*, as it is a part of creation.

- Where do you go in nature for consolation? How has nature healed your body, mind, and/or spirit? What does "belonging together" contribute to this consolation and/or healing?
- In the long quote above this practice in *Nature as Spiritual Practice,* Hildegard describes a woman who has "no greenness in her strength." What does Hildegard mean by this? How would you evaluate the "greenness in your strength"?
- Parker Palmer describes the human soul as being in many ways tough and resilient, yet also shy and reclusive. How is *viriditas* similar or different from these qualities of the human soul?
- Slow yourself, balance yourself, and be yourself in any way that is best for you. Recall Thomas Merton's idea that simply consenting to be what you are (human, tree, mountain) gives glory to God. Pray the green, the *viriditas,* as a way of giving this kind of glory to God.

PRACTICE 12.3

Healing Dialogues and Wondrous Exchange²

A Lakota medicine woman may address a stone as *Tunkashila* ("Grandfather"). Similarly, the Omaha may address a rock with the respect and reverence that one pays to an ancient elder. Thus they may address a rock as, for instance:

> Unmoved
> From time without
> End
> *You rest*
> There in the midst of the paths
> *You rest*
> Covered with the droppings of birds
> Grass growing from your feet
> Your head decked with down of birds
> *You rest*
> In the midst of the winds

2. This practice is taken mostly from Bill Plotkin, *Soulcraft: Crossing into the Mysteries of Nature and Psyche* (Novato, CA: New World Library, 2003), 167-69.

You wait
Aged one.[3]

INTENTION The intention of this practice is to help us hear the earth "rumbling and straining" and to sharpen our reciprocal perception by participating in the language of the earth, a language of healing. If you have never traded speech with a lizard, a rattlesnake, an elk, a desert juniper, the wind, or a rock, you have a world-shifting treat in store for you.

PRACTICE In this practice you will discover that you have thousands of new relatives, fascinating and wild and true. Most modern people would feel foolish to sit and talk with a snake or a tower of rock. Most nature-based people (such as the Lakota and Omaha above), in contrast, would feel great sorrow for anyone who could not talk with a snake or communicate with a bear, or hear the song of trees or the language of rocks.

- Go wandering outside. Anywhere. Bring your journal. Be prepared to offer a gift: a poem, grief, yearning, joy, your eloquence, a song, a dance, a lock of hair, praise, tobacco, water. Early on, cross over a physical threshold (such as a stream, a large rock, a passageway between two trees) to mark your transition from ordinary time and space to the sacred. While you are in this sacred space, do not eat, do not speak with other humans, and do not enter any human-made shelter.
- Wander aimlessly until you feel called by something, not through your strategic, thinking mind, but called rather through your intuition. Hear a call (it may be very faint at first) and follow it. It may be a bush, a blade of grass, a stone, an anthill, a lizard, maybe a vulture or a rotting animal carcass. Whatever it is, sit and observe it closely for a good length of time. Interact with your senses, imagination, your faith, hope, and love. Perhaps offer a gift at this time.
- Now introduce yourself, out loud — yes, out loud. This is important. Tell this other being about yourself. Be prepared to follow the conversation for an indefinite period of time, perhaps a half hour or more. First tell it why you have been wandering around waiting to be called; tell it your motivation for being there. Tell the truth, your deepest, most intimate truth. Tell it what it was that attracted you to it. In addition to ordinary human language, you might choose to speak with song, poetry, non-

---

3. Cited in David Abram, *The Spell of the Sensuous: Perception and Language in a More-than-Human World* (New York: Pantheon Books, 1996), 71.

verbal sound, images, emotion, or body language (movement, gesture, dance).

- After you have told this subject in nature all about yourself, using the same speech options, tell this other everything you notice about it. Describe its features, again out loud and respectfully; tell it what interests you about those features, about what you find attractive about it. Keep communicating until it interrupts you.
- Stop and listen. Listen with your ears, eyes, nose, skin, intuition, feeling, imagination (aural, visual, kinesthetic, and so on). Listening ("direct, pre-reflective perception," as Abram calls it) is different from your own psyche fabricating metaphors (such as a tree "telling" you to stand tall), but the latter is okay too. It may take hours before you get interrupted. Or days. Or it may never happen. Or it may take only the time for a deer to blink its eye.
- Keep the conversation going several rounds. In your journal, record and/or draw what happens. As with the examples above from the Omaha people, speak and/or write down how you would like to address it — how it can be addressed with reverence.
- As you go, offer the other your gratitude and a gift, if you haven't already. When you are ready, return to the place of your original threshold and cross back over.
- A conversational relationship of this kind with even a single tree will fire dimensions of your own wildness, your soul, that might not have been unleashed through even the closest or most exotic human relationships. Be prepared for these.
- In the future, enter your conversations with all others with the same respect you would give to, say, Abraham, Sarah, or some other ancient person from Scripture. And don't be surprised if at times you discover more about yourself than you do about the other!

PRACTICE 12.4

Christ's Cosmic Exchange: Astronomy Picture of the Day

O fire ever blazing!
The soul who comes to know herself in you
finds your greatness wherever she turns,
even in the tiniest things,

in people
and in all created things,
for in all of them she sees
your power
and wisdom
and love.

                                Catherine of Siena, Prayers (P 12)

INTENTION   The intention of this practice is — by using pictures of the universe that were captured by NASA and are available online — to gain perspective on infinite distance and infinite intimacy, and to explore Calvin's "wondrous exchange" initiated by Christ, seen and experienced on a cosmic scale.

PRACTICE   NASA has a wonderful website called the "Astronomy Picture of the Day." In this practice you will have an opportunity to meditate on truly unimaginable (but not infinite) distances, allow them to become part of the seed growing into a "beautiful tree," and reflect on Christ as the bridge from self to God and from self to these images, even in their mind-boggling distances. These pictures of creation, in balanced and healthy ways, draw us out of ourselves and into Christ, who is intimately near yet stretches as a bridge to infinite distance — and back into infinite closeness.

- Go to NASA's website, Astronomy Picture of the Day: http://antwrp
  .gsfc.nasa.gov/apod/astropix.html, or go to the Archive of Astronomy
  Pictures: http://antwrp.gsfc.nasa.gov/apod/archivepix.html.
- Spend time as you would in nature with the "picture of the day," or go
  through the archive pictures. In either case, simply let your imagination absorb the "unimaginable" distances, complexities, beauty, changes, time, and light of these pictures of creation.
- Find your own bridge to reverence: that is, find your own way — it may
  be through prayer — to acknowledge the mystery, wonder, power, goodness, and beauty of these images. You may want to print some of the pictures or save them. You may promise yourself to spend some time at night away from light pollution and wonder at the night sky.
- The Creator of these objects is both in and beyond them; yet Christ is a
  bridge through them to the God of intimacy. Journal or draw or let a lingering thought creatively imagine such a bridge.
- Likewise, Christ the bridge spans the distance between you and these

objects of creation. What attributes or images of God help you walk this Christ-bridge?
- Take time to thank Christ for the beauty and wonder of these brilliant distances and the equal beauty and wonder of his intimacy. How do these beauties and wonders heal your soul? Allow the pictures and the objects they represent to seep into you as part of the sacred temple of Christ.

PRACTICE 12.5

Talking Circle: Nature Healing
[Full practice also in *Nature as Spiritual Practice*]

INTENTION   The "talking circle" is a simple yet powerful tradition found in a variety of cultures and religions. Its power is in its simplicity.[4] The talking circle is based on the idea that everyone has something of value to say and something of value to learn. Using the talking circle format, we intend in this practice, within a group, to find healing connections with the natural world.

PRACTICE   This is a practice meant for a group of people who have come together with a common expectation: connective, healing relationships with the creation. The purpose of the gathering is to let all express experiences of intimacy, healing, solace, or guidance in nature.

- Participants form a circle, sitting or standing.
- A facilitator, as a model of what might be spoken, begins the conversation. After speaking, the facilitator passes a "speaking stone" or feather or some other object that has special meaning to the group. The facilitator passes the "speaking" object to the person next to him or her, and so on around the circle.
- The ground rules for the talking circle are:
  - Only the person holding the "speaking stone" may speak.
  - Each person may speak for as long as he or she wishes, or not at all.
  - There is no cross-talk; each person gets one opportunity to speak as she or he holds the "speaking stone" and only speaks at that time.

4. This practice is based loosely on "The Talking Circle," in Carl A. Hammerschlag and Howard D. Silverman, *Healing Ceremonies: Creating Personal Rituals for Spiritual, Emotional, Physical and Mental Health* (New York: Perigee, 1996), 145-51.

> – The information shared in the circle should be held in confidence, unless all participants agree to do otherwise.
- Topics for speaking are up to the person holding the "speaking stone" and might include:
  - Experiences of healing in nature
  - What in nature needs healing
  - Prayer for the healing of nature
- The talking circle is a way to have all participants involved in the process, trusting the setting and the Spirit to draw out each individual's truth, thus making it a part of the community's truth as well.
- The group may observe other rituals as a ceremony, or the "speaking stone" may be passed around the circle a number of times with the invitation to speak to different aspects of healing.
- When the circle is completed, the facilitator can pause for a moment of silence, then give a short word or phrase of thanks for something in nature. Then the group passes the stone as before, allowing each person to give the same short prayer of thanks for a particular object or sensation or grace from nature.
- It is appropriate to end with a prayer for healing and guidance by and for creation.

The Moral Senses of Nature

CHAPTER THIRTEEN

Spiritual Practice as Moral Response

PRACTICE 13.1

Considering Lilies

INTENTION The intention of this practice is a slight addition to Abba Sisoes's response to the brother: "It is no great thing to be with God in your thoughts, but it is a great thing to see yourself inferior to all creatures" — *and to act accordingly.* Thus we will begin contemplating our moral response to nature by considering the lilies of the field.

PRACTICE Seeing the "earth as it is" is a practice of attention that transforms perception. It also transforms ethics, lifestyle, and the energy for and will to do ecological action.

Read Luke 12:22-29, focusing particularly on the lilies of the field. As you read, imagine you are with Jesus as he is speaking. For this part of the practice, you may choose either to quiet yourself indoors or out. Find that still place within you as you imaginatively reenact the scene.

- Take time to still yourself before entering into an imaginative encounter with Jesus. Then —
  - Imagine that you are one of the disciples.
  - Imagine your relationship up to this point with Jesus. Use anything you know about him to draw yourself into his presence. What does he look like? Hear his voice, notice his smell, remember a meal you shared together, words he has spoken.

– Imagine the other disciples around you. You are happy to be with Jesus and these other men and women. You have seen things you do not fully understand, but you are drawn powerfully to this man, how he knows your needs and desires, how he looks at you with intimate compassion.

– Sit down in a field with the other disciples, because Jesus has suggested a rest. Notice that you are sitting in a beautiful setting, a meadow. It is warm, but not unpleasantly hot. You talk a while among yourselves. Imagine or experience odors, sights, and feelings.

– After some conversation, Jesus draws your attention to the flowers you see strewn across the meadow. Their colors radiate from the greens of the meadow. Jesus says, "Look at those lilies in that field, how they grow: they neither toil nor spin." You have never looked at lilies in this way before. Neither toiling nor spinning, they are still perfect just as they are. They are very good at simply being lilies.

– Imagine that you are like the lilies Jesus is pointing to, that you, like they, are cared for.

– Stay with the lilies just as they are, enjoying the simple presence of the moment.

– After a time, Jesus asks you personally, "Where are you most yourself?" "When are you satisfied simply in being yourself?" Answer him.

– After a time, Jesus stands and invites you to walk with him. You walk beside him, simply talking about things like the lilies and how they live and about what you "see" and how you "act" toward the natural world when you are most like the lilies, most like yourself.

– What virtues does nature bring to mind — not virtues in the sense of "shoulds," but virtues as responses based on creation's own imperative of care?

– Talk with Jesus about what you notice and how you might more mindfully tend to and care for the earth. Listen to his reply.

PRACTICE 13.2

Bread and Wine

[Full practice also in *Nature as Spiritual Practice*]

INTENTION To evoke a moral response to nature equivalent to the response of receiving the bread and the wine.

PRACTICE   We receive the bread and the wine out of our own freedom, and yet they are gifts that actually create and reciprocate freedom.

- During the next few times during Mass or Eucharist or Lord's Supper, notice how you receive the bread and the wine. What does your reception and partaking of them mean to you? What do you experience?
- Noticing your experience of the elements, also consider and wonder at the fact that both bread and wine are themselves pure elements of creation. Jesus could have made any number of things into sacraments representing his body and blood. Why did he choose bread and wine?
- What does it mean to you that the body of Jesus Christ is a part of nature, a part of creation?
- A few attributes of a moral response to nature at any time include humility, compassion, kindness, perseverance, hospitality, mindfulness, and love. Find a personal response to nature that is similar to or even recreates your response of receiving the bread and the wine. Act on that response.

PRACTICE 13.3

Nature and Moral Discernment

INTENTION   Given the complications of determining an appropriate moral response to nature, the intention of this practice is to apply a model of discernment to the natural world that grounds moral response in contemplation, prayer, and love.[1]

PRACTICE   In his book *Discernment and Truth,* Mark McIntosh envisions five modes of discernment, "always springing from a contemplative mode, extending forth in a practical mode, and always returning to the contemplative." He plots these five modes and their relative location in the rhythm between the active and contemplative life in the following way:

1. The material that follows in this practice, excluding the questions at the end, is adapted from Mark A. McIntosh, *Discernment and Truth: The Spirituality and Theology of Knowledge* (New York: Crossroad, 2004), 5-22.

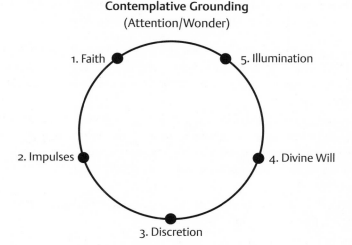

Contemplative Grounding
(Attention/Wonder)

1. Faith

5. Illumination

2. Impulses

4. Divine Will

3. Discretion

Active Practice
(Attention/Wonder Manifested)

McIntosh does not make a direct link between creation and grounding or practice, but we will apply these five modes that way in this practice. Read the five moments of discernment below and McIntosh's explanation of their interrelationships. Following those are questions that will help you apply your moments of discernment to nature.

1. Discernment as *faith*: spiritual discernment as grounded in a loving and trusting relationship with God (see Rom. 12:2 and John 14–17, where Jesus is training disciples to participate in the ever-sharing relationship Jesus has with the Father and the Spirit).

2. Discernment is distinguishing between good and evil *impulses* that move people (see Paul's exhortation in Rom. 12:2 and the material in 1 Cor. 12:10 on fruits of the Spirit and "discernment of spirits").

3. Discernment is *discretion*, practical wisdom, moderation, and generally good sense about what to do in given practical situations (see Paul in Rom. 12 again; see Prov. 8:12, 17; and see the material on fruits and gifts of the Spirit, p. 134 below).

4. Discernment as sensitivity to and desire to pursue *God's will* in all things (see John 5:30; 12:50; 15:12-15).

5. Discernment is illumination, contemplative wisdom, a noetic relationship with God that *illuminates and facilitates knowledge* of every kind of truth (see Col. 3:8-11, primarily concerning contemplative wisdom).

Of the relationship of these aspects of moral discernment, McIntosh writes: "Moments (1) and (5) are the most contemplative and transformative. Moment (2) discerns the 'whence' of life, the impulses or spirits that move one. Moment (3) is the most practical; yet such a disposition toward sound judgment depends on the previous moments in order to act with discretion in any given situation. Moment (4), the 'whither,' bespeaks the crucial teleological dimension of the whole discerning life, for if one's life (taken individually or communally) is not consistently pressing on toward the meaning and truth of all reality in terms of God's intention for the whole, then every act of discernment easily becomes short-circuited, falling captive to smaller, meandering desires."

- How have you experienced each of these five moments in the natural world? What in nature has taught you each of these lessons?
- How have these lessons in nature led to discretion?
- If you have not encountered any of the five moments in the natural world, why do you think that is? What is blocking you from such an encounter? Do you experience these moments strongly in other settings, such as with friends, at work, in worship, in social action or justice?
- In what moment are you the "strongest" and in what the "weakest"?
- Since this is a "dynamic" model of discernment, how do you see these various moments moving organically through your life? How do they move through nature?
- How do you experience in your life the dynamic circle between contemplative grounding and active practice?
- Use each of these moments to formulate an active response to an ecological issue that deeply concerns you.

CHAPTER FOURTEEN

Transforming Perspectives and Earth Insights

PRACTICE 14.1

Divine Provision and Human Degradation

[Full practice also in *Nature as Spiritual Practice*]

INTENTION   The intention of this practice is to attend to, pray over, and respond as needed to seven divine provisions laid out in Scripture that make the earth a livable, self-sustaining, health-giving environment, and seven corresponding degradations that humans have imposed on these divine provisions. The practice is effective whether done in solitude or with a group, though a group will lend a variety of perspectives.

PRACTICE   Calvin B. DeWitt lists seven *God-given* "provisions of creation" and seven *human-created* "degradations of creation," each biblically based.[1] Holding the degradations and the provisions together functions in itself as a contemplative exercise that can lead in turn to organic moral responses to earth-needs.

- Notice and attend to each of the divine provisions and human degradations listed below. Attend first to one provision, then concentrate on its corresponding degradation. Visit locations of as many of both as you

1. Calvin B. DeWitt, "Creation's Environmental Challenge to Evangelical Christianity," in *The Care of Creation: Focusing Concern and Action*, ed. R. J. Berry (Leicester, UK: InterVarsity Press, 2000), 60-73.

are able and find out as much as you can about the genesis of each (especially the degradations).

- DeWitt gives biblical support for each of the divine provisions. Where do you find in Scripture that God has provided these gifts? Spend time in creation with these gifts, imagining what God intends in providing each of them.
- In prayer, first pray about the goodness, beauty, plentitude, and giftedness of the world as God has provided it. After this, pray about how we have degraded so many of these gifts and contemplate active ways to heal them. In the midst of this prayer, leave some quiet time to listen for and/or imagine how God is speaking to you about these same issues. Do not be hesitant to tell the earth how you feel and how you are talking with God about it. This, too, is prayer.
- It has been said that vocation is where the needs of the world intersect your own gifts or deepest longings. How are the needs of the earth, your own gifts, and God's guidance calling you to respond to earth-pain?

Provisions of Creation: Upon which all creation, all creatures, and all human life depend. Many are celebrated in Psalm 104:[2]

1. Regulation of earth's energy exchange with the sun, which keeps earth's temperatures at a level supportive of life through the long-standing greenhouse effect, and which protects life from the sun's lethal ultraviolet radiation by filtering sunlight through the stratospheric ozone layer.
2. Biogeochemical cycles and soil-building processes, which cycle oxygen, carbon, water, and other vital materials through living things and their habitats and build life-supporting soils and soil structure.
3. Ecosystem energy transfer and materials recycling, which continually energizes life on earth and incessantly allocates life-sustaining materials.
4. Water purification systems of the biosphere, which distill, filter, and purify surface waters and the ground water on which all life depends.
5. Biological and ecological fruitfulness, which supports and maintains the rich biodiversity of life on earth by means of responsive and adaptive physiologies and behaviors.
6. Global circulations of water and air, which distribute water, oxygen,

---

2. DeWitt, "Creation's Environmental Challenge," 62.

carbon dioxide, and other vital materials between living systems across the planet.

7. The human ability to learn from creation and live in accordance with its laws, which makes it possible for people to live sustainably on earth and safeguard creation.

Degradations of Creation:[3]

1. Alteration of earth's energy exchange with the sun, which results in accelerated global warming and destruction of the earth's protective ozone shield.

2. Land degradation, which destroys land by erosion, salinization, and desertification, and reduces available land for creatures and crops.

3. Deforestation, which annually removes some 100,000 square kilometers of primary forest — an area the size of Iceland — and degrades an equal amount by overuse.

4. Species extinction, which witnesses the elimination of more than three species of plants and animals from the earth each day.

5. Water quality degradation, which defiles ground water, lakes, rivers, and oceans.

6. Waste generation and global toxification, which result from atmospheric and oceanic circulation of the materials that people inject into the air and water.

7. Human and cultural degradation, which threatens and eliminates long-standing human communities that have lived sustainably and co-operatively with creation, and also eliminates a multitude of long-standing varieties of food and garden plants.

PRACTICE 14.2

A Creation Rule of Life

INTENTION Monastic communities and lay communities and individuals practice a "rule of life" to orient their work, prayer, and community toward God. The intention of this practice is to create and commit to practicing a "creation rule of life" that orients us toward God without neglecting the basis of the rule: creation itself.

3. DeWitt, "Creation's Environmental Challenge," 61-62.

PRACTICE   This practice helps us begin to think about and act upon what we see around us. As explained in the text, ethical ecological action is also Christian practice. This practice will help us transform our experiences of nature into practices for the health and sustainability of the planet by developing a "rule." "Rule" comes from the Latin *regula,* which simply means a "straight line," or a straight path. If the word "rule" seems a bit strong for you, use "rhythm" or "intention" instead.

- Since any rule of life should be based on the passions, desires, and longings that God has placed within you, begin by making a list of:
  - Things that nurture your mind, body, and spirit in creation
  - Positive aspects of your relationship with creation
  - Don't censor yourself
  - This is your unconscious creation rule of life
- First, divide your list into the following categories, interpreting each category in the context of nature, noting where you have gaps and where your desires tend to congregate:
  - Seeking God
  - Work
  - Study
  - Spiritual community and worship
  - Care of your body
  - Service to others
  - Hospitality
  - Relationships
  - Transformation
- Now group your list according to Thomas Berry's three categories (described in the text) by deciding how each item in your list is the best example in nature of:
  - Differentiation
  - Subjectivity
  - Communion
- Finally, with each passion, longing, and desire that is a natural part of your make-up, use these lists to determine how you can be intentional about dedicating your actions and work in creation to God. In other words, how does your own and your community's organic practice in nature inform how you will live in sustainable companionship with creation? The lists from the community that bases its creation rule of life on Berry may give you some ideas.

- Rules are sometimes difficult to keep. Here are nine guidelines for developing a "creation rule of life" that will help keep your own rule "sustainable":
  - Listen to your heart's desires when discerning the rule. God often speaks to us through our deepest longings.
  - Make sure that your rule includes some joy, play, and fun.
  - Take baby steps. Don't make your rule impossible to follow.
  - Baby steps are good, but give yourself a bit of a challenge, too.
  - Figure out how much structure you need — a lot or just a little.
  - Learn to pay deep attention to your practices as you do them — whatever they are — which will help prevent boredom.
  - Find someone or a community of people to communicate with and to keep you accountable about your rule — or even to join you in a similar rule of their own. It is easy for us to fool ourselves about all kinds of things.
  - Read your rule regularly. It is easy for us to forget what we begin to dislike or what becomes difficult.
  - Sometimes you're going to have trouble keeping your rule, especially when the wounds of creation seem larger than your small ability to address them. Recognize that you're human, that others are working with you, and try again.

The Green Beatitudes

Wisdom and the Green Beatitudes

Scripture's Green Designs
[Full practice also in *Nature as Spiritual Practice*]

INTENTION The following practices use Scripture as a basis for fostering contemplative attention, seasoned discernment, reciprocal perception, the capacity to wonder, and moral response appropriate both to others and to creation. Each practice comes with a minimum of instruction or questions: the intention is that each reader and practitioner will find his or her own ways into Scripture's green designs and continue to experience creation as spiritual practice leading to contemplative attention and moral action — here — "on earth as it is."

PRACTICES The following practices consist of suggestions from Scripture on how to grow in ways that are congruent with Scripture's own green intentions. Some are much more than suggestions: they are gifts, ways of life, models for growth in communion and love of nature. Normally these suggestions are not applied to the natural world, but as you meditate on them in the context of nature, you will find that the application of these gifts and virtues is more than appropriate.

"Joy" is one example from the list of "fruits of the Spirit" in Galations. If we equate joy with praise, there is no question that many parts of creation are less in a position to praise than they once were and we, in turn, less able to pray as a result. But perhaps in another sense green praise in the midst of a brown ecology reminds us that the Spirit groans in prayer when we cannot. As overwhelmed by ecological destruction as we may be, prayer still rises up from the earth — if not in praise, then in lament. This, too, may be a prayerful "gift of the Spirit."

For each of the following practices, allow yourself to wander or hike or stroll or sit or simply stand in the natural world — in a city park, along a beach, in a state park, into the wilderness, or in a garden — noticing and attending to each Scripture suggestion in turn as it helps you reflect on nature and what nature might be able to tell you. You may find, say, a gift of the Spirit in nature, or nature may show you a gift of the Spirit in yourself or others you have not noticed. Keep in mind that the lists and individual items are simultaneously ways of contemplating creation and paradigms for loving, caring action in nature.

- *Gifts of the Spirit: Galatians 5:22-26.* Where in nature do you find each gift? How does nature mediate the following gifts of the Spirit to you? Taken as a whole, how would practicing the gifts of the Spirit form the way we live in the everyday? Let nature share these gifts with you: "If we live by the Spirit, let us also be guided by the Spirit" (Gal. 5:25).
  - Love
  - Joy
  - Peace
  - Patience
  - Kindness
  - Generosity
  - Gentleness
  - Self-control

- *Gifts of the Spirit of the Lord: Isaiah 11:2.* Again, allow yourself to attend to these gifts in the natural world and to note how the natural world, in turn, shares these gifts with you.
  - Wisdom
  - Understanding
  - Counsel
  - Might
  - Knowledge
  - Fear of the Lord
  - Delight in the Lord

- *Spiritual gifts: 1 Corinthians 12:8-10.* The spiritual gifts of 1 Corinthians are in many ways shorthand for how the natural world forms and shapes identity. Perseverance and patience in perceiving these gifts in nature

and receiving them through nature will slowly build your understanding of their function in nature.
- Utterance of wisdom
- Utterance of knowledge
- Faith
- Healing
- Working miracles
- Prophecy
- Discernment of spirits
- Various kinds of tongues
- Interpretation of tongues

- *Two kinds of wisdom: James 3:13-18.* James uses two kinds of wisdom. "Wisdom from above" is reminiscent of the Proverbs text: "Does not Wisdom call, and does not understanding raise her voice?" (Prov. 8:1). "Wisdom from below" gives insight into some of the human "foolishness" that contributes to ecological stress and degradation. Do you see "wisdom from below" in nature herself?

Wisdom from Above	Wisdom from Below
Gentleness born of wisdom	Bitter envy
Purity born of wisdom	Selfish ambition
Peaceable	Earthly [in the sense that it is self-
Gentle	centered, rather than God-
Willing to yield	centered, insubstantial]
Full of mercy	Unspiritual
Full of good fruits	Devilish
Without partiality	Disordered
Without hypocrisy	Wickedness of every kind
Yields a harvest of	
righteousness sown in peace	

- *The Ten Commandments: Exodus 20:2-17.* Though the Ten Commandments, like the other Scripture suggestions, are predicated on a contemplative attentiveness in order to help us see a situation or relationship clearly, they are a bit different from all the suggestions given previously. Unlike the previous lists, the Ten Commandments are a list of things *not to do* instead of a list of gifts or things *to do.* Both can be applied to the natural world; both help us to be conscious of how the natural world mediates Christ's guidance to us; both move from aware-

ness to intention to action. Applying each, how do the Ten Commandments help you "hear" Wisdom's voice in creation? Some people prefer
or find the Green Beatitudes more helpful; others will find that the
following Green Ten Commandments speak more intimately and
meaningfully.

- You shall have no other gods before me.
- You shall not make yourself an idol.
- You shall not misuse the name of the Lord.
- Remember the Sabbath.
- Honor your father and your mother.
- You shall not murder.
- You shall not commit adultery.
- You shall not steal.
- You shall not give false witness.
- You shall not covet a neighbor's goods.

- *New life in Christ: Colossians 3:2, 12-17.* The description of the new life in
  Christ given in Colossians returns us to the opening section of this
  chapter, summed up by Saint Hesychios in the epigraph to chapter 13:
  "Watchfulness is a graceful and radiant virtue when guided by Thee,
  Christ our God." Here the contemplative watchfulness and the life of
  virtue blend together, as both are guided by Christ. Do you find places
  in nature not bestowed with the garments of this new life of Christ?
  Why?
  - Set your minds on things that are above.
  - Clothe yourselves with:
    - Compassion
    - Kindness
    - Humility
    - Meekness
    - Patience
  - Above all, clothe yourselves with love.
  - Bear with one another.
  - Forgive one another.
  - Let the peace of Christ dwell in you richly.
  - Teach and admonish in all wisdom.
  - Sing psalms, hymns, and spiritual songs.
  - Do everything in the name of the Lord, giving thanks to God.

A Sample Retreat

Nature, Scripture, and Christian Practice

> *Christianity is an out-of-doors religion. From the birth in a grotto at Bethlehem to the crowning death on a hill of Calvary, all of its important events took place out-of-doors. All of its great words, from the sermon on the mount to the last commission to the disciples, were spoken in the open air. How shall we understand it unless we carry it under the free sky and interpret it in the companionship of nature?*
>
> Henry Van Dyke, *Out-of-Doors in the Holy Land*[1]

The practices in this retreat are intended as introductory exercises that will help participants become comfortable with processes of Christian formational identity in nature. In this retreat the practices use personal memory and Scripture to serve as familiar points of entry from which to begin the lifelong transformational process of nature as spiritual practice.

If you are facilitating the retreat, read over the material at the beginning of the *Field Guide* or in *Nature as Spiritual Practice* about group spiritual practice and the processing of practices. These materials will help you facilitate a retreat that finds the proper balance between the planning and the unexpected surprises nature will bring your way as she joins you in fa-

---

1. Henry Van Dyke, *Out-of-Doors in the Holy Land: Impressions of Travel in Body and Spirit* (New York: Charles Scribner's Sons, 1908).

cilitating the retreat. Read through the practices closely and become familiar enough with them so that you can explain the details to the participants, and perhaps most importantly, know them well enough to know when moving away from the stated practice will enhance the experience of the retreat. Remind retreat participants that each practice is a point of entry into lifelong practices with nature.

Start each practice with a suitable prayer, and read the practice aloud to the group. Emphasize that the "intentions" for each practice are only that: if nature moves them in another direction, be sure they understand that that is to be expected and encouraged. Give participants a schedule of the complete retreat, and plan time for resting, wandering, and free time for prayer and reflection — whatever participants would need to do to make the retreat most meaningful and to open themselves to nature and God.

Ritual, Music, and Prayer

Organize the retreat as if it were a liturgy or ritual you would like to participate in. Provide music at the beginning and between practices. Opening with relaxation exercises, breathing practices, meditation, and a short liturgy of worship focused on nature may suit your purpose. Provide places for small groups to discuss their experiences in private and a space for the group as a whole to gather. Music, meditation, and other rituals are appropriate between practice sessions. How you end the retreat is important. One good way to end is to form a circle and pass around the "speaking stone" (or feather). Whoever is holding the stone or feather is allowed to speak whatever he or she wants to related to his or her experience with the retreat. You may suggest that, as the stone or feather is passed around, participants complete phrases such as "Nature led me to . . ."; "I was able to praise God during this retreat through nature best when . . ."; "God was present for me in nature when . . ."

Length of Retreat

This retreat can be done as a one-day or two-day retreat. The suggested time frames here are for a one-day retreat. You can adjust them to fit your own two-day retreat. Whether you take one or two days, be sure to factor in plenty of time to process the practices in small groups and together as a larger group to explore patterns of experience or themes that arise during the practice. As in all retreats, give retreat participants plenty of extra time between exercises to explore on their own, or in small groups. Invite them to "wander" in nature at their own pace. Whether the retreat is one day or two days, additions are always appropriate: hymns with nature themes, worship focused on the God of creation, or even a particular discernment process your group gathers around using nature as a guide.

Altering Practices

Always be open to new insights or unexpected experiences that can alter practices to make them even more appropriate for your group. If a particular practice is described for an individual, adapt it for your group.

Materials Needed

Bibles for each participant; journal notebook or writing paper with pens/pencils for each participant; a copy of each practice for each retreat participant.

PRACTICE 1

Remembering Nature

INTENTION   The intention of this simple practice is to awaken your early and current memories of a relational connection to nature.

PRACTICE

- Our memories preserve, among other things, a record of how God has been present and has blessed us in creation. This practice helps us recall times and places where creation has guided, taught, and comforted us. Honor the wisdom of memory through a prayer of thanks to God for creation.
- A good way to do this practice with others is to divide into groups of four. Allow each member to talk for five minutes, uninterrupted, in response to the questions or statements below. If members stop speak-

ing during their allotted time, simply wait; after a few moments of silence, they will usually start again. After each person has had an opportunity to speak for five minutes, allow each group of four to share together any thoughts or memories or issues that came up during the time of individual speaking.

- Recall and describe your first memory of nature. Who were you with, or were you alone? Is this early memory a positive or negative memory?
- Imagine, write, or share a place in nature where you love to go and why.
- In the last week, what have you experienced of nature — an incident, a news item, a dream — that caused you pain (physical, psychological, emotional, or spiritual)?
- In the last week, what was something you did or made or saw that was connected to nature and made you glad to be alive?
- Recall, write, or share an experience in nature where you felt the presence of God.

PRACTICE 2

Scripture: An Out-of-Doors Book

INTENTION   Nature plays a decisive role in moving us ever closer to God. The intention of this practice is to begin to sense that movement by reading Scripture in a new way. Perhaps Scripture is meant to be read outdoors!

PRACTICE

- With your Bible, wander outdoors in creation until you find a place in the natural world that "calls" you, a place where you will be assured of some privacy.
- As you find your place — as it "calls" you — perform a small ritual in recognition of crossing into sacred space. This can be very simple: cross a creek, pass by a stone, walk across a field or through a gate, pass under a canopy of branches, move from sun into shadow, or actually create a line in the ground with your foot or with stones that you then step across. As you perhaps say a short prayer, you are acknowledging that you are entering sacred space in any of these ways.

- When you have found your place, settle in and pay close attention to what is going on around you. Notice the plants, the trees, the soils and grasses, birds, sounds and smells, colors, movements, water. Note and enjoy whatever happens to capture your attention in this environment.
- Take your time: acknowledge in your own way that everything around you was created by God and is sustained by this same Creator.
- When you feel that you "know" your surroundings well, sit down (if you are not already), and pick a Scripture passage to read. You may want to choose a favorite passage, a new passage that you just happen to open to, or you may think of one that seems appropriate to the place and moment. One suggestion is Psalm 104.
- Begin to read the Scripture passage slowly, out loud. As you read, pay attention not only to the content of the passage — its story or meaning — but also to the effect of the Bible's words and your voice on your surroundings. How do you imagine creation itself is hearing the words of its own Creator? How do you experience the words spoken out-of-doors?
- Stop when you like; listen to the silence; notice and watch for signs of how creation hears the Word in this silence.
- Also take time to notice your body and your own inner feelings. How are you experiencing Scripture, in body, mind, and spirit, as you read aloud in nature?
- Notice how the words rise out of silence and fall back into silence.
- In what ways do you share with nature the "hearing" of these words?
- Leave with a quiet, short prayer of praise or thanksgiving for God's Word and for the temple of the creation that has embraced you during this time.
- As you cross back over or pass your marker of sacred space, know that you are carrying something sacred from creation back into "normal" life.

PRACTICE 3

Reconnecting: Be the Thing You See

INTENTION   In this practice, via contemplative openness and attention, we begin to reconnect with nature by letting nature "speak" as we listen to her language and read the "book of nature." Using all of our perceptions, feelings, and thoughts, the intention is to reconnect with nature and, as the poet John Mofitt says, "be the thing you see."

PRACTICE   This is a fairly simple practice on the surface, but a practice that asks us to reconnect with nature by listening more deeply than is our custom. It is an invitation to listen or read below the surface of things. You will need a journal notebook or writing paper and pencil or pen. [Times can be adjusted to fit your retreat.]

- [About 10 minutes] Walk attentively and/or sit contemplatively, letting the natural world capture your attention. Begin to focus on something to which you can give your full attention: a leaf, stones, a branch, flowers, seeds, bark, soil, a tree, sand, waves, a cloud you can observe while lying on your back.
- [About 10 minutes] Stay with this object and examine it as closely as you can, using all your senses. Notice also how this object is connected to the rest of creation. For instance, notice how what may have initially appeared as a simple brown branch is actually splotched with grey-green lichen, or that the bark is many shades of "brown," from deep yellows to hidden purples. You may concentrate on the texture of the branch, how light brightens or shadows ridges and valleys within the branch, perhaps the uniform or unique angles at which smaller branches, buds, or leaves project from the branch. The longer you linger, the more you will see and "read."
  - When you have finished "listening" to (or "reading") nature, take time to write down eight or ten words or phrases that describe the object, or how you feel in relationship to the object. Write these fairly quickly and spontaneously without censoring yourself. You might want to write single words, short phrases, or even make a few quick sketches.
- [About 15-20 minutes] Now give yourself this time to write about this object and its place in creation, using as many of the descriptive words from above that you can. Write anything you like: how you feel in relationship to the object; words or phrases that are descriptive of the object; memories the object evokes. You may prefer to do a poem rather than a prose piece, but make it your own.
- This is a good practice to do in a group setting. Allow people the times allotted above, and have them reconvene for about thirty minutes. Form small groups of three to five people wherever you would like. Invite all the members to read what they have written. Give everyone time to adjust to the group, particularly those who are reluctant to

share their thoughts. Let as many read as are willing to; those who choose not to read may wish to summarize their experience. Allow the group to respond to the writings, but without judgment. Refer to the author not by name but as "the writer" (see the preface to this book for more guidance in appropriate group interaction).

- Whether in solitude or with a group, reflect on how "becoming what you see" reconnects you to the natural world.

PRACTICE 4

Scripture: Our Book of Creation

> For you shall go out in joy, and be led back in peace; the mountains and hills before you shall burst into song, and the trees of the field shall clap their hands.
>
> Isaiah 55:12

INTENTION Creation is ubiquitous in Scripture; it is on every page. As we begin to read Scripture with an eager heart for creation, we begin to find that creation is patiently traced, lovingly embraced, alternately kind and wrathful, but always a central character in the drama that forms the people of God. The intention of this practice is to begin to reclaim nature as an essential component of formational identity as found in Christian Scripture.

PRACTICE Open the Bible anywhere and look for images or intimations of creation. Read closely, noticing whatever you can find.

- Begin to expand your vision of creation in Scripture. Some of what you will find is obvious; much of it will require "new eyes."
- For instance, every mention of "mother" or "father" or "child" is a reference to creation. Lineage and ancestors and the nations they form are a major part of Scripture and a part of creation.
- Peoples move through creation, often from a land, through a land, to a land.
- Place is declared sacred and stones are erected; people die, are buried in the earth, and their place is remembered; bushes burn yet are not consumed; clouds enfold mountains; a child is born in a humble place. Actively imagine the landscapes in which Scripture stories take place.
- Praise and song are not only human prayer: they are ways of prayer in which every element of creation participates. Creation, as John Calvin

says, is sustained by God in part through these prayers of praise and song. The first verse of Psalm 96 reads: "O sing to the Lord a new song; sing to the Lord, all the earth." Find other instances of nature praising the Creator (a few examples are Pss. 95–99, 100, 104, 148, 150).

- Time and space, light and dark, movement and stability, orientation and dimension, heaven and earth are all parts of creation. Reread the two creation stories at the beginning of Genesis.
- Jesus' words and teachings show that he paid careful attention to the natural world. Water, bread, and wine were central to his mission. Deserts drew him. Lakes and inland seas provided moments of refuge, fish for meals, lessons in fear and trust. Mustard seeds and mountains focused and supplied meaning to his parables. Stars, sheep, gold, frankincense, and angels played a central role in his very human birth. Take time to notice how Jesus interacted with nature and drew constantly on nature for his teaching.
- In Jesus' passion and death, the drama of redemption is played out within the context of creation: palm leaves, thorns, roads, hills, crowds, iron nails, wood, blood, sour wine, hyssop, broken bones, abandonment, the earth shaking, rocks splitting, darkness, myrrh and aloes, spices, gardens, tombs, large stones, dawn, terror and amazement. At the center of this drama, death itself is also a part of creation. And now, resurrection from the dead is a part of creation as well.
- From the beginning of Genesis to the end of Revelation, creation brackets and contains the story of the people of God. Creation is a part of the alpha and omega of Scripture that point to Christ. Continue to read and marvel at the innumerable ways in which nature is central to the drama of the Bible.
- At the most fundamental level, every word in Scripture, whether spoken, written, read, heard, or enacted, is a part of creation.
- Begin noticing how creation affects decisions, aspirations, emotions, ambitions, humility, blessings, sin, hope, families, travels, communities, faith, love, ancestors and lineage, and individuals within the stories. Notice that these very things (decisions, aspirations, emotions, etc.) are themselves a part of creation.
- I have randomly opened my Bible to Daniel 2:31. Daniel is interpreting a dream: "You were looking, O king, and lo! There was a great statue. The statue was huge, its brilliance extraordinary; it was standing before you, and its appearance was frightening." What can we see of creation in this verse? First, though we don't often grant them the status,

dreams are themselves gifts of creation. The very first word refers to creation: to have a "you," first we must have a creation. "Looking" requires created will, created eyes, created interpretation. "There" is a place in creation; the "statue" is a human creation, presumably created out of stone of some kind. "Huge" is only possible in the context of a creation that contains dimension and comparison. "Standing" organizes space around us and thus helps us orient ourselves within creation. "Appearance" requires light, which was the first element of creation out of the chaos of nothingness; and "brilliance" is a reflection of light. "Frightening" is an emotion brought about in us and is a part of the natural world. And this is all "only" a dream.

- Notice that as you begin to read Scripture in this way, it comes more alive. You begin to enter into Scripture as you would enter Scripture as prayer, which, of course, it is. This opens a door, in turn, to connection and belonging within nature that itself can become a lifelong prayer.
- The most ecologically and erotically lush book in all of Scripture is no doubt the Song of Songs. It can be read as a kind of primer on reading Scripture as a book of creation.
- This is a lifelong practice, but as you leave this practice today, spend time with God, inviting God into all that you notice and love about nature.

PRACTICE 5

Breath and the Name of God

INTENTION   One way to reconnect with nature is to experience the Hebrew word *ruach* (meaning breath, wind, or spirit) in a tactile way, connecting wind in nature with the breath or Spirit of God. This practice can be done in almost any outdoor setting: your backyard, in front of your office, in a park, walking down the street, in deep wilderness, during retreat.

PRACTICE

- Pause from your thinking and the business of everyday life.
- Outdoors, bring your awareness to the feel of God's breath — that is, the wind — moving around your skin and body. The atmosphere is always moving, even if this motion is barely perceptible.
- Notice how nature's breath is touching you. Depending on the

strength and consistency of the wind, its touch may feel gentle, firm, playful, or rough.

- Turn your face toward the wind, open your arms wide, embrace the wind, and feel it in your hair and skin and clothes. Spend time experiencing the breeze or wind as divine breath.
- Some rabbinic teachers refer to the very sound of the Tetragrammaton, the "nameless name" for God — YHWH (Yahweh) — as the sound all humans make as they breathe. Listen to your own breath. Open your mouth as you breathe and feel the air move in and out of your body. You will notice the inhaled breath is cooler than the exhaled air, which releases breath warmed by your body. Begin to listen to your breath passing in and out of your body. If you listen closely, you will hear it, the name of God: the inhale is "yah," the exhale is "weh," the name of God — softly, over and over. With each breath you are actually speaking the name of God, and in that sense your very breath is constant prayer. Let the wind, your breath, and the air surrounding you connect you to God.
- Notice that all animals are breathing the same way. As we know, plants also breathe, in a kind of reverse way of how animals breathe: they inhale carbon dioxide and exhale oxygen. Sit with the plants around you and any animals or birds you see as they breathe in rhythm with the divine breath.
- Finally, breathe in the air deeply and then whisper thanks. This sacred, tangible breath, this *ruach*, makes possible our own life-sustaining respirations.

Close this retreat with prayer from the Psalms and praise from each participant.

- All participants gather in a circle and read the following:

Lord, in wisdom you have made them all; the earth is full of your creatures. . . . Praise the Lord! Praise the Lord, sun and moon; praise the Lord, you shining stars!

Ps. 104:24; 148:1, 3

- Pass a "speaking stone" or feather around the circle. As all participants hold the stone or feather, invite them to praise the Lord as well by repeating the following phrase and completing it with a subject of their choice from creation: "Praise the Lord for . . ." Pass the stone or feather around the circle until all have had a chance to praise the Lord with creation. End with a suitable closing prayer.